RECOLLECTIONS OF
GREAT GARDENERS

RECOLLECTIONS OF GREAT GARDENERS

Graham Stuart Thomas

FOREWORD BY JOHN SALES

FRANCES LINCOLN

To Margaret Heal, who by her impeccable typing has made readable the manuscripts of so many of my books, this book is dedicated with affection and best thanks.

Frances Lincoln Limited
4 Torriano Mews
Torriano Avenue
London NW5 2RZ
www.franceslincoln.com

British Library Cataloguing in Publication data
A catalogue record for this book is available from the British Library.

ISBN 0 7112 2288 6

Commissioned and edited by Jane Crawley
Designed by Anne Wilson
Consultant editor Tony Lord
Printed in England

2 4 6 8 9 7 5 3 1

The essays on Gwendolyn Anley, Gertrude Jekyll, Arthur Tysilio Johnson
and Lady Moore are reprinted from *Cuttings from My Garden Notebooks* by
permission of Sagapress Inc., U.S.A., 1997. 'Arthur Tysilio Johnson' first
appeared in *Hortus*, and 'Lady Moore' in *Moorea*, the journal of the Irish
Garden Plant Society.

All the illustrations in this book are taken from
The Complete Flower Paintings and Drawings of Graham Stuart Thomas (1987)
by permission of Sagapress Inc., U.S.A.
HALF-TITLE PAGE: *Prunus mume* 'Omoi-no-mama',
Iris unguicularis and *I. u.* 'Mary Barnard'
FRONTISPIECE: *Anemone* x *hybrida* 'Prinz Heinrich' and
A. x *h.* 'Honorine Jobert'

BY THE SAME AUTHOR
The Old Shrub Roses
Colour in the Winter Garden
Shrub Roses of Today
Climbing Roses Old and New
Plants for Ground-Cover
Perennial Garden Plants: The Modern Florilegium
Gardens of the National Trust
Three Gardens
Trees in the Landscape
The Art of Planting
A Garden of Roses
The Compete Flower Paintings and Drawings of Graham Stuart Thomas
The Rock Garden and its Plants
An English Rose Garden
Ornamental Shrubs, Climbers and Bamboos
The Graham Stuart Thomas Rose Book
Cuttings from My Garden Notebooks
Thoughts from a Garden Seat
Recreating the Period Garden (editor and contributor)

CONTENTS

Foreword by John Sales   10

Overture   44

THE GARDENERS   59

The Lord Aberconway • *Bodnant, Colwyn Bay, North Wales*   60

Cuthbert H.D. Acland • *Stagshaw, Ambleside, Cumberland*   62

The Amorys • *Knightshayes Court, Tiverton, Devon*   65

Gwendolyn Anley • *St George's, Woking, Surrey*   70

Hugh Armytage-Moore • *Rowallane, Saintfield, Co. Down,
Northern Ireland*   76

Lt.-Col. Sir Edward Bolitho • *Trengwainton, Penzance,
Cornwall*   80

Edward Augustus Bowles • *Myddleton House,
Enfield, Middlesex*   83

Major Henry R. Broughton, Second Baron Fairhaven
Fairhaven Woodland and Water Garden, South Walsham, Norfolk   88

Huttleston Broughton, First Baron Fairhaven
Anglesey Abbey, Cambridgeshire   90

Sir James and Lady Burnett of Leys • *Crathes Castle,
Kincardineshire, Scotland*   93

Warwick and Phyllis Deeping • *Eastlands, Weybridge, Surrey*   96

Ralph Dutton, Lord Sherborne • *Hinton Ampner, Alresford,
Hampshire*   99

Leonard and Dorothy Elmhirst • *Dartington Hall,
Totnes, Devon*   102

Betty Farquhar • *Ardsallagh, Tipperary, Eire*   104

Reginald Farrer • *Ingleborough, Yorkshire*   106

Mark Fenwick • *Abbotswood, Stow-on-the-Wold,*
  Gloucestershire   109

Ruby Fleischmann • *Chetwode Manor, Buckingham*   112

Dr Wilfrid Fox • *Winkworth Arboretum, Godalming, Surrey* 114

Frank Galsworthy • *Chertsey, Surrey*   116

John S.L. Gilmour • *Cambridge University Botanic Garden,*
  Cambridge   118

The Earl and Countess of Haddington • *Tyninghame,*
  East Lothian, Scotland   121

Sir Harold Hillier • *Ampfield House, Romsey, Hampshire*   123

Christopher and Betty Hussey • *Scotney Castle,*
  Lamberhurst, Kent   125

Collingwood ('Cherry') Ingram • *Benenden, Kent*   127

The Earl and Countess of Iveagh • *Pyrford Court,*
  Woking, Surrey   129

The Honourable Robert James • *St Nicholas,*
  Richmond, Yorkshire   131

Sir John Jarvis • *Hascombe Court, Godalming, Surrey*   134

Gertrude Jekyll • *Munstead Wood, Godalming, Surrey*   135

Sir Geoffrey and Susan Jellicoe and John Humphris
  Sutton Place, Guildford, Surrey   139

Arthur Tysilio Johnson and Nora, his wife
  Bulkeley Mill, Ty'n-y-groes, North Wales   142

Major Lawrence Johnston • *Hidcote Manor,*
  Chipping Campden, Gloucestershire   150

Frank P. Knight • *Knap Hill Nursery, Woking, Surrey*   154

Major and Mrs Knox Finlay • *Keillour Castle,*
   Perthshire, Scotland   158

The Marchioness of Londonderry • *Mount Stewart,*
   Newtownards, Northern Ireland   160

Vera Mackie • *Guincho, Co. Down, Northern Ireland*   163

L. Maurice Mason • *Talbot Manor, King's Lynn, Norfolk*   165

Bernard Maxwell • *Steadstone, Dalbeattie,*
   Kirkcudbrightshire, Scotland   167

Sir Herbert Eustace Maxwell • *Monreith,*
   Wigtownshire, Scotland   169

Kenneth and Douglas McDouall • *Logan, The Mull of*
   Logan, Wigtownshire, Scotland   171

The Messels • *Nymans, Handcross, Sussex,*
   and Birr Castle, Co. Offaly, Eire   174

W.J. Mitchell • *Westonbirt Arboretum, Tetbury,*
   Gloucestershire   178

Mary Louise, Duchess of Montrose • *Brodick Castle,*
   Isle of Arran, Scotland   181

Lady Moore • *Willbrook House, Rathfarnham, Dublin, Eire*   183

Heather Agnes Muir • *Kiftsgate Court, Chipping Campden,*
   Gloucestershire   190

Sir Harold Nicolson and Vita Sackville-West
   Sissinghurst Castle, Cranbrook, Kent   194

Harold Ainsworth Peto • *Iford Manor, Wiltshire*   197

Phyllis Reiss • *Tintinhull, Yeovil, Somerset*   199

The Rentons • *Branklyn, Perth, Scotland*   201

William Robinson • *Gravetye Manor, East Grinstead, Sussex*   205

James P. C. Russell • *Sunningdale Nursery, Windlesham,*
    Surrey   209

Molly and Noel Sanderson • *Ishlan, Ballymoney,*
    Co. Antrim, Northern Ireland   212

Sir Eric Savill, Thomas Hope Findlay and John Bond
    The Savill Garden, Windsor Great Park, Berkshire   214

David Shackleton • *Beech Park, Clonsilla, Co. Dublin, Eire*   217

Tim Smit • *Heligan Gardens, Mevagissey, Cornwall*   220

Dr B.T.D. Smith • *Sidney Sussex College, Cambridge*   222

Constance Spry • *Winkfield House, Windsor, Berkshire*   225

Sir Frederick Stern • *Highdown, Goring-by-Sea, Sussex*   230

Lord Strickland • *Sizergh Castle, Kendal, Cumbria*   233

Thomas Upcher • *Sheringham Park, Norfolk*   235

Charles Paget Wade • *Snowshill Manor, Stow-on-the-Wold,*
    Gloucestershire   237

The Walpoles • *Mount Usher, Co. Wicklow, Eire*   238

The Warburgs • *Boidier, Headley, Epsom, Surrey*   241

Sir Clough Williams-Ellis • *Plas Brondanw, Porth Madog,*
    Gwynedd, North Wales   243

Ellen Ann Willmott • *Warley Place, Great Warley, Essex*   244

Conclusion   248
Index   254

FOREWORD
Recollections of Graham Stuart Thomas

GRAHAM THOMAS'S RECOLLECTIONS are his characteristically precise and personal record of most of the leading gardeners of the middle part of the twentieth century. Almost all stem from his gardening friendships and professional contacts. These were often one and the same because he made it his business to cultivate the most accomplished in the field. Like his writings about plants, each is a well-observed and well-remembered account, owing nothing to the opinions of others. While never likely to be comprehensive, they amount to a fascinating review of the social and professional circle of the man who, perhaps more than anyone, has shaped the development of gardens and gardening since the Second World War.

My recollections of Graham Thomas are intended as a complementary tribute to the gardener who was probably the most influential of our age. First as his assistant and then as his successor as (Chief) Gardens Adviser to the National Trust (while he continued as part-time consultant), I knew him personally and professionally for over thirty years. Others will emphasize one or another of Graham's many talents or his work as a nurseryman. My account is based entirely on my personal experience of his relationship with the gardens of the National Trust, which became the centre of his life and the workshop for his writings.

Almost single-handedly Graham Thomas invented historic garden conservation in Britain. Never, before the National

Trust, had anyone or any body assembled gardens and landscape parks so as to preserve their essential qualities for ever, for everyone. No one had tried to do it and no one knew whether it could be done.

The Trust was forty years old before it acquired its first significant garden, Montacute, in 1937 and over fifty by the time it decided, with Hidcote, to accept gardens on their own merits, quite apart from the quality of the house and estate. By 1954 the Trust already owned an unprecedented selection of some of the greatest gardens that this country of great gardeners had created during the previous three hundred years. But most of these – like Blickling, Cliveden, Killerton, Stourhead and Wallington – had come with a great house and estate.

After appointing John Workman as its first Forestry Adviser, the Trust decided that its gardens, even more subject to continuous change and decay than its woods, needed regular guidance. As a result Miss Ellen Field, from Burghclere, was appointed as the Trust's pioneer (part-time) Gardens Adviser, starting in June 1954. But tragically, within less than six months, she died following a road accident while driving back to Exeter from Cotehele. One can only speculate as to the extent to which the course of twentieth-century garden history might have been different had she lived.

Graham Thomas was appointed as part-time Gardens Adviser in the spring of 1955 at an annual salary of £400. Having been employed at T. Hilling and Co. since 1931, rising to become manager, he had unsuccessfully applied to become the first Director of the Royal Horticultural Society's garden at Wisley, the job going to Frank Knight. Thomas saw the Trust as an opportunity to become involved with some of the world's greatest gardens and perhaps as a means of furthering his emerging career as a writer. Part-time at the

Trust he certainly was, simultaneously continuing his work at Hilling's and at Sunningdale Nursery until 1971. Incredibly, the longest he ever worked for the Trust was for nine months of the year, in the late 1960s, when there were between sixty and seventy gardens to visit. In winter he 'hibernated' to write his books.

Although by 1955 the Trust owned several other gardens, Graham Thomas was called upon at first to advise on only seven – Blickling, Montacute, Sheffield Park, Hidcote, Cotehele, Killerton and Stourhead; not a bad bunch by any standard. Never enjoying holidays in the modern sense or weekend breaks without a purpose, Thomas filled his free time advising at these seven gardens. To begin with he was taken around and introduced by the Trust's Chief Agent, Hubert Smith, to whom he answered, and then left alone to get on with advising directly each of the area agents and head gardeners.

With characteristic thoroughness, unbending persistence and good-humoured patience Graham Thomas soon established a style of advising that has been followed effectively and developed by gardens advisers ever since. Discussion was confined entirely to those responsible for running the garden – especially head gardener, managing agent and gardens adviser – diligently covering all parts and aspects of the garden. He focused almost entirely on gardening – renovation, planting, pruning, felling, adjustment, adaptation and good husbandry – and was reluctant to involve himself in technical matters, management, machinery and wider issues generally. In the sense of choosing and associating plants suitable to the place, taste was always an underlying consideration.

As far as possible joint decisions were teased out on the spot or deliberately deferred to be raised at the next visit, priority being agreed for important jobs. As a result everyone had an opportunity to have their say and take part in making decisions, large and small. It is difficult now to imagine the poverty of the National Trust at that time. Every property was short of funds and extreme care had to be taken to husband resources, especially of labour.

Julian Prideaux, lately Deputy Director-General and a former land agent and regional director, recalls how Graham Thomas 'was always punctual, reports were timely and well written – firm handwriting on thin duplicate book paper' and that 'the homework had been done'. He was remarkably quick and economical in producing his reports, which were always comprehensive, accurate and prompt; indeed he would usually write them in the evening and triumphantly present them to the managing agent next morning. As a result no one could easily forget the discussions and work could go ahead immediately. It has been known for head gardeners to have a quiet word with their staff after the morning tour and for the adviser to come back after lunch to find a job discussed earlier already done.

These written reports acted as a guide for all but routine work until the subsequent visit and provided a means of checking progress between one meeting and the next. As a series the reports were a way of identifying recurring problems on matters like standards, staffing, funding and attention to detail. In retrospect they also provided a valuable record and now form an important archive.

Thanks to Thomas's tact, willingness to listen and ability to provide an answer to almost any gardening problem, after some understandable apprehension on both sides, effective working relationships developed almost everywhere. Gardeners soon began to look forward to the adviser's visits as a day for showing what had been achieved and as a way of raising and resolving difficult problems. This was true even in the potentially difficult circumstances of advising at places like Lyme Park in Cheshire which was managed by the local authority.

Geoffrey Moon, head gardener at Wallington for many years, recalls that an important element of the adviser's visits was what he learned in the process. 'He taught me how it was important to look at detail ... a plant of the wrong flower colour that had crept in • where slugs were chewing away at the artemisia.' He learned 'to walk around all areas of the garden regularly and observe' and that 'head gardeners must see the garden as a whole'. Graham Thomas would often bring plants from his own garden and Geoffrey Moon says, 'At my home in Cambo in a little border at the front door I have a fern which was given me by Graham Thomas. I see it every day and remember him with great affection and count myself incredibly lucky to have had such a wonderful mentor and good friend.'

The consistent application of this process of regular critical appraisal and review has been the basis, no less, of the Trust's reputation for high standards and attention to detail, combined as well with long-term vision.

By this steady incremental improvement and renewal maximum use would be made of slender resources. Inessentials were eliminated to concentrate attention on what was perceived at that time to be most important. In this way the continuity of inevitable change, development and decay in gardens was matched by a consistent process of adjustment, adaptation and renewal, always anticipating future change and reacting to unforeseeable events like storm, flood, drought and disease.

Thomas's reports were models of economy and precision in the use of words. Philip Cotton, head gardener at Cliveden for many years, admired his efficiency. 'A few days after the visit I received a typewritten report. Everything which had been agreed was in it, down to the smallest detail, clearly stated and unambiguous. Graham Thomas has always been meticulous and demands the same standards from those around him.' Latterly at Mount Stewart the visit would last two days and the report would consist of several pages of close-packed notes tersely couched as instructions but always prefaced by a short but beguiling introduction to the effect that 'the following is my advice'. Looking back, Nigel Marshall, head gardener for thirty years, says, 'His visits to Mount Stewart were an education for me. He had a great eye for detail, very exacting in his requirements regarding plants for particular places. He was a master of colour schemes ... on one of his visits he sketched out his "colour wheel", most valuable when organizing colour schemes.' Peter Borlase, formerly head gardener at Lanhydrock comments, 'With all his vast knowledge, he was never above listening to one's point of view.'

As a fledgling gardens adviser in 1971, and after I succeeded him in 1973, I learned a great deal from being lucky enough to accompany the great man on his visits. But I was never allowed to be a passenger, frequently being put on the spot for the answer to a problem, horticultural, technical or managerial, or asked to give an instant suggestion for a plant to fulfil a particular role, a game at which he was the undisputed champion. There was more than a hint of horticultural one-upmanship about Graham.

When it came to commenting on my reports, as well as having an eagle eye for botanical exactitude, he was adept at making tactful and always relevant suggestions for improvement and economy. Occasionally his zeal for precision in language would exceed normal usage – 'I expect you realize that "decimate" means the removal of one in ten,' and 'I suppose you remember that "scruffy" means infected with the scurvy?' On the other hand he would write about 'slim garden staffs' where there were few gardeners and 'single-handed gardeners', raising the image, in my mind anyway, of the Trust's gardens being staffed by one-armed anorexics.

In those early days most advisers worked from home and when we were contemplating a move from Chelmsford to Cirencester, to be more centrally situated, Graham politely enquired whether I had considered the problems of travelling from the west in the morning and back in the evening with the sun in my eyes both ways.

Graham Thomas was always immaculately turned out – brown, heavy shoes (always clean), black umbrella (neatly furled), jacket and tie (very conservative), raincoat (ancient but respectable). In his own words he was 'very particular' about most things and one of his particularities was the habitual flower in his lapel, which one was expected to comment upon and (fail to) identify precisely. Peter Borlase recalls, 'He would always have a button-hole ... rose 'Cécile Brünner' or a bud of 'Niphetos'. Puzzled as to how at the end of a long day the rose was as fresh ... he revealed his secret by turning over the lapel of his jacket ... a silver phial filled with water.'

In a similar vein there were certain rituals and habitual jokes attached to each visit. He would often bring a thoughtfully chosen plant or some seeds; there would be comments at some places about 'always bringing rain'; he would ask kindly after the family; he never forgot anything from the previous visit; at some places there was a game of 'spot the plant' – those 'inappropriate subjects' that the head gardener may have 'popped in'. On the other hand he had a tactful way of declining the offer of a plant which he did not want for his own garden. He would say quite firmly, 'No, it looks lovely in *your* garden.'

He was always 'Mr Thomas' to head gardeners except at Cliveden where after twenty-five years advising he suddenly suggested that Philip Cotton should call him 'Graham'. Any gardener who inadvertently addressed him as 'Graham' would be politely but firmly put down there and then. As Philip Cotton says, 'This sense of propriety was exhibited . . . when I suggested that my assistant head gardener be included in the party to tour the garden. "No," he said, "we pay you to do this job and no one else." '

Perhaps the most important ritual involved tea, and everyone quickly became aware of his partiality for cakes and biscuits. Archie Skinner, former head gardener at Sheffield Park says, 'He particularly liked my wife's home-made scones.' When tea time was in danger of being omitted from the schedule he would politely point out the need for the property's tea room to be 'inspected for quality and service'. At Cliveden his habitual excursion into Cookham for lunch was explained by the quality of the home-made cakes at the Copper Kettle. He always bought a cream sponge to take home.

Graham Thomas was invariably courteous and disarming, being remembered not only by many head gardeners and other staff but also by tenants and donor families as 'the perfect gentleman'. He disliked protracted discussion and would usually head off any serious argument by deferring the matter, often with a joke. As a last resort he would say, slightly testily, 'No doubt you will do what you think fit' and close the discussion. But he was also persuasive and persistent, knowing exactly when to give way on a point of detail or to include a plant he would not otherwise think right in order to win on the bigger issues as he saw them. Archie Skinner remembers suggesting a group of winter-flowering *Viburnum* x *bodnantense*: 'The garden is closed when they are in flower,'

Thomas replied ... then later, 'You and your staff would enjoy them; let's do it.'

Gardens advisers encounter the whole range and extraordinary diversity of people involved with the work of the Trust – donors, tenants, committee members, volunteers and staff at all levels. Inevitably there were differences of priority, clashes of taste, even occasional rudeness, but Graham Thomas would always argue constructively and retain his composure. I cannot recall him raising his voice or losing his dignity. Looking back Anthony Mitchell, historic buildings representative in Severn Region says, 'In a crisis he was a tower of quiet strength. An awkward tenant (there were very few) or a mad prospective donor (more than a few) was very firmly, but courteously, dealt with.' His patience was tested by people he considered argumentative, ignorant and insensitive but most of all by discursive discussion heading to no clear conclusion – 'time wasting'; in such circumstances he could be impatient, even a little waspish. He quickly made up his mind about people. When I was appointed in 1970 without seeing Graham Thomas, my introduction was principally a walk round his garden at West End, where I was asked to identify a few key plants, including *Rhododendron yakushimanum*. At the end I could see 'You'll do' written across his face.

He was extremely good with children and made lifelong friends with several of the families who hosted him on his travels. Christopher and Francesca Wall, with whom he often stayed both on the Attingham estate and in their house at Bradenham, from 1962 for over twenty-five years, speak glowingly of his eagerly anticipated visits. Given his routine of tea on arrival, a 'rest' to write notes, a timely meal and early to bed, he was the perfect guest who always made time for the children. In the Wall household Thomas was known as 'Mr

Tom-bush' after their son's first efforts at saying his name. 'He was much loved.' Arland and Sylvia Kingston recall, 'When our children were small Graham took much delight in teaching them card games, particularly Newmarket. They gained a bit of a reputation as card-sharpers at a very early age.' Despite this he was in demand as a godparent for the children of staff with whom he stayed. He was also a keen supporter of a local private school when he lived at West End, near Woking.

As far as children in gardens were concerned he took a practical and sensibly selective, if unfashionable, approach. He rightly suggested that some gardens, because of their fragility and restricted spaces, were unequivocally not for children. There were others where children should be welcome provided they were firmly under control of teacher or parent. Purposeful recreation was his creed and woe betide the parent of any child he came across casually kicking a football around a National Trust garden.

This resolute attitude to recreational time was a character trait which seemed to control the way Graham Thomas organized his life, including his advisory visits. There was a fixity of purpose about all he did whether he was working, entertaining or relaxing. Not for him the aimless dreaming of the romantic or the impulsive fecklessness of the spendthrift. He organized money and time in a strictly economic and conservative way. There were so many ways to employ his many talents and he seemed driven, if not wholly by a work ethic, at least by a compulsion to use every moment to good effect, including conversation. He took careful notes of amusing events and stories and was never short of a jokey anecdote or an apt quotation. He had a well-cultivated sense of humour, a quality essential for success with any gardens adviser. Scorning television, he was no couch potato and never listened to the radio on his long car journeys – 'This is when I do my thinking.'

He was undoubtedly an accomplished musician, playing the piano and singing, mostly madrigals. His musical taste penetrated the nineteenth century, but not the twentieth. Graham loved opera and the male voice especially. Gerard Noel, former regional agent in Wessex, says he 'definitely thought of himself as musical … to hear him whistling was like hearing someone very bad at trying to play on a bent saw.' Had he known Gerard's opinion (and I feel sure he did not) he would certainly have worked hard to bring his whistling up to the standard of his other musical skills.

Nicolas de Bazille Corbin, as regional agent for East Anglia, remembers Graham Thomas's visit in September 1955, the first of many occasions when he stayed at Aylsham Hall, on the Blickling estate, the grandest house for a land agent in the Trust. Here, after a strenuous day of garden visiting he would 'invariably play the boudoir-size grand piano' and sometimes sing madrigals. Laurence Harwood, East Anglia assistant agent in the 1960s, played the cello and has vivid memories of making music with Graham Thomas and of evening excursions to Gresham's School at Cromer, where they formed a quartet 'with Mrs Vawser and Gerald Shaffrey'.

Not that he always, or even usually, preferred to stay with regional staff and he never stayed with a head gardener. Although he got on well with most staff he would accept invitations to stay only where the house was spacious and where the evening routine (including meals) suited his demanding schedule, affording him time and comfort to write notes and get to bed at his usual early hour. He tended to avoid smokers' houses, places where the lifestyle was informal or unpredictable, and the company of big dogs. He would refuse to share a car with a ('smelly') wet gundog or with someone who insisted on smoking. There was always a 'no smoking' sign in his car, long before it was socially acceptable to ban cigarette smoking. A curious contradiction to this would be at a few places where flies were a nuisance in the garden where he would bring out a packet and smoke a cigarette to ward them off.

Among his several well-cultivated sensibilities was an acute and discerning sense of smell. He was an expert at describing odours of all kinds, distinguishing the subtle fragrances of old rose cultivars with comparative ease. The rotting leaves of *Cercidiphyllum japonicum* were 'like strawberry jam', *Iris graminea* flowers 'like plum pudding' and *Salvia turkestanica* 'like barmaids' armpits', although I never discovered how he found this out. All the more surprising then that he should prefer to stay in an hotel at Betws-y-coed where the charming lady proprietor kept cats and which smelt so strongly feline that I vowed never to join him there, even for a meal. As Graham himself would say, 'For those who like that sort of thing it is just the sort of thing they like.'

Of Graham's many qualities two stand out as important in his work as a gardens adviser – his power of observation and his ability to visualize. Perhaps partly because of his experience as a botanical artist, he was particularly good at observing detail, while taking in the wider picture. As a result he missed nothing in the small scale but also noticed gradual deterioration in the garden as a whole. This is a crucial role of the gardens adviser, whose fresh eye is vital. Another indispensable quality of a gardens adviser is the ability to design with time and space as well as with plants: the capacity to visualize the effects of felling and planting over time and their impact on spaces and views. Because of his ability as a draughtsman, with a few lines Graham Thomas was able quickly to sketch the scene, Repton-style, 'before and after' and so convince tenants, donors and colleagues of the need for often radical and far-reaching proposals.

His approach to landscape and garden planting was indeed strongly picturesque. He tended to see gardens and landscape parks with a painter's eye as a series of pictures and views, almost with an invisible frame around each. This approach was highly effective in encouraging others to use their eyes and in establishing guidelines for views, colour schemes and other special effects. But it played down the sense of the visitor experiencing the garden from within, as part of it. While Graham's sketches to illustrate proposals for park planting, for instance at Attingham Park, were brilliantly conceived as prospects from particular points, movement and animation were always at most subsidiary. 'You must look from here,' he would say.

Similarly the precision of his planting schemes was fine when everything developed according to plan but left little margin for error or accident. Particularly in the wider landscape, plantations need constantly to be manipulated to achieve a desired effect and a broad-brush style at the outset can be the best approach. We cannot avoid having to trust the eye of our successors, something Graham was reluctant to do.

As befits the role of the National Trust as the greatest conserver of gardens in the world, Graham Thomas's attitude to gardens was essentially conservative, making the best of things, often after many years of decline, within the constraints of poverty and reduced staffing. In the 1950s and 1960s, with a comparatively small membership of less than a quarter million and few paying visitors, in some gardens the Trust could not always afford basic necessities, like effective machinery and greenhouse heating and repair. Plants could hardly be afforded and exchanging between gardens was often the only way forward, resulting inevitably in a degree of repetition from garden to garden. Graham Thomas was adept at making a great deal out of comparatively little, targeting resources where they would be most effective and teaching the art of frugal gardening.

In those days, before the Garden History Society was formed and before English Heritage (as it now is) became serious about gardens, there were no models to follow, no body of knowledge about caring for historic gardens. Furthermore there was precious little research to hand. Graham Thomas had to feel his way, gleaning as much as was known about each place from available records and discussions with former owners and staff, supplemented by his acute observation of clues on the ground. Priority was given, as he put it, 'to making every garden presentable' (in other words well cared-for), improving standards pragmatically and enriching the planting gradually so as to attract visitors and give them a satisfactory experience.

The uninhibited exercise of one's own taste was not at the time considered to be in any way inappropriate in historic gardens. Graham exercised his impeccable Jekyllian good taste widely but also, ahead of his time, he valued Victorian and other period styles, appropriate to the place but not always popular among aesthetes and the current country house set.

In the 1950s, 1960s and 1970s the Trust exercised its own brand of understated elegance almost as a corporate style. This seemingly effortless good taste tended to be exercised universally throughout the Trust's properties and was widely admired, becoming the distinctive mark of its high standards. Its application was the preserve of committee members and staff in the Historic Buildings department who alone had the necessary background and aesthetic sensitivity. It was inconceivable that a gardens person should be able to understand or exercise anything as subtle and restrained, even Graham Thomas, who had not yet acquired iconic status. Head priest of good taste was Robin Fedden, as Historic Buildings Secretary a highly influential person in the National Trust. Graham did not have an easy time but gradually he proved his point as the Trust's approach to style became more educated and diverse.

Graham Thomas was above all a plantsman of astonishing knowledge and range, much of his expertise having been gained by personal experience and observation. His horticultural interest began with small plants, hence his eye for detail, and he had this extraordinary ability to explore primarily the minutiae of a place while absorbing bigger issues and generalities at the same time. This talent and a cautious approach suited the circumstances. Notions of 'historic gardening' hardly existed until the early 1970s and most of his planting had to be intuitive, aiming to pick up the traditions of the place and counter the unjust but common jibe about 'the dead hand of the Trust'.

Of course at this distance, in retrospect, it is possible to question some of Thomas's work – repetition of certain ornamental trees and plants, overanxiety to extend the season of interest, too much Jekyll-style planting, frequent 'tasteful' colour schemes, too many old roses, a tendency to overcrowd and overwork. But in the circumstances of the 1960s any or all of these might have been imposed even by the most caring of historic garden owners. Compared with his contemporaries working in historic gardens like Lanning Roper, whose distinguished work was instantly recognizable, Graham Thomas's planting schemes were self-effacing, picking up the traditions of the place to a considerable degree.

It is extraordinary that so little was destroyed, and so few schemes have needed to be unpicked, bearing in mind the rapid increase in garden history research and the consequent development of understanding and expertise in historic garden conservation in the last quarter of the twentieth century. The fact is that he was in the vanguard of conservation thinking and practice for at least twenty years. Furthermore some of his innovations and adaptations, especially his borders, have become historically significant in their own right. Even under the Trust gardens have to move on.

After the formation of the Garden History Society in 1965 and thanks in no small measure to the influence of the Trust's gardens, interest in historic gardens developed. As well as an historic buildings secretary in head office, the Trust employed regional historic buildings representatives (now 'curators'). These were honorary at first, but as the work became more demanding professional appointments were made, eventually increasing to two in most of the sixteen regions. Their role as experts on the history of each property, protectors of character and 'guardians of taste' eventually included the garden. From the mid-1960s working relationships were gradually established to include the historic buildings representative as well as the managing agent and head gardener. Generally this was accomplished without creating too much of a committee and in most instances the partnerships were creative as well as providing checks and balances. The Trust was having to become more accountable.

Probably the first serious historicist garden recreation in England, Moseley Old Hall, arose after 1962 out of a partnership between Graham Thomas and Christopher Wall, historic buildings representative based at Attingham Park. Encased in Victorian brickwork, the seventeenth-century house had been acquired because of its connection with Charles II after the Battle of Worcester in 1651. Its garden consisted of a derelict former piggery and smallholding and there was no record of a garden on the site. Something had to be done and

Robin Fedden, Historic Buildings Secretary, called upon Ralph Dutton, author of *The English Garden* (1937) and creator of Hinton Ampner, and Miles Hadfield, garden historian and author of *Gardening in Britain* (1960), who was fostering a growing interest in garden history at the time. Hadfield's consequent visit with Thomas and Wall led to an imaginary seventeenth-century garden materializing almost there and then, using elements copied from contemporary books, including a tunnel arbour, knot garden, nut walk and orchard. The bones of Hadfield's rudimentary layout were fleshed out by Graham Thomas with the Trust's first attempt at period planting, while Christopher Wall dealt with the structures. Since then the garden has been further developed and remains an important milestone in garden history terms as well as continuing to enrich the visitors' experience.

A similar attempt to recreate a garden appropriate to the house but unsupported by any historical evidence was made at the moated sixteenth-century Little Moreton Hall in the early 1970s. The idea and the general layout were inspired by Graham Thomas, who then left me, as a new boy, to work out the scheme – including a yew arbour and a simple enclosed knot reflecting the patterns on the romantic black-and-white house. With a generous grant from the Leverhulme Trust, the way was clear for the subsequently appointed assistant adviser, Paul Miles, to draw up the final plan and supervise the work.

Like Graham Thomas, Miles Hadfield was a founder member of the Garden History Society and became its President from 1971–77. As such he was an influential figure in persuading the Trust to accept Westbury Court, Maynard Colchester's derelict seventeenth-century water garden, with buildings but no house. The garden had miraculously survived since the time of William and Mary. Indeed with its canals, tall pavilion and horticultural emphasis, it was a 'rare and beautiful' example of a modest garden with Dutch influence. Restoring Westbury Court was a courageous act of faith by the Trust and another important milestone in historic gardening, being the first serious attempt at comprehensive historic garden restoration in Britain, using the maker's account books of 1696–1705, combined with evidence remaining on the ground. Graham Thomas and Anthony Mitchell, historic buildings representative, were enthusiastic pioneers of garden restoration but there were serious financial difficulties for the regional agent, Colin Jones, to overcome. Compared with modern restoration the whole thing was done on a shoestring, with no archaeology and a greatly simplified layout. The long west wall, knocked down by the developer whose plan to develop the site for housing was thwarted, had to be rebuilt three courses lower to save money.

Perhaps Westbury Court's most effective head office ally was Lord Rosse, chairman of the Properties Committee, a man of immense charm and tact as well as vision. It was he who arbitrated a dispute about planting, in favour of Miles Hadfield's and Anthony Mitchell's view that only plants introduced before 1700 should be used, while tactfully allowing Graham Thomas, who wanted to use 'suitable plants', to put some eighteenth-century old roses in the little walled garden, which in fact was an eighteenth-century addition. Still valid, Thomas's argument was that 'authenticity' in gardens is virtually impossible without knowing every detail like the type of turf; also without reverting to all the original horticultural practices – grass cutting, vegetable cropping, pruning and training; in other words, without the original labour force. Later as chairman of the putative Gardens Panel as well as the Properties Committee, Lord Rosse was hugely influential in promoting gardens and supporting schemes of recreation, restoration and renovation at places like Little Moreton Hall, Ham House, Felbrigg and Ickworth.

Graham Thomas was a strong proponent of the idea of restoring that part of the Claremont estate which was owned by the Trust. It is a garden that incorporates the whole development of the eighteenth-century English Landscape style. Although by then I had succeeded him as (Chief) Gardens Adviser, he continued with Claremont, amongst other gardens, for several years as a consultant. One of the Trust's three comprehensive restoration schemes of the 1970s, along with Erddig and Ham House, the work had to be carried out, as at Ham, unduly quickly to comply with the terms of the gift of funds from the Slater Foundation.

The restoration of Claremont depended on a dedicated team, led by the managing agent Peter Mansfield, advised by Graham Thomas and the historic buildings representative Martin Drury, later Director-General, who frequently arrived late. (Peter Mansfield writes, 'I suspect it was G. who in a waspish moment referred to Martin Drury as "the late Mr Drury".') This huge scheme demanded historic survey and research at breathtaking speed and simultaneous clearance and restoration; also frequent urgent decisions on the spot and complicated strategies for incorporating car park, restaurant and service areas. Above all it required great courage to peel off a deep blanket of *Rhododendron ponticum* without knowing precisely what would be revealed. It was Lord Blakenham, as chairman of the Gardens Panel (and a former Cabinet Minister), who bravely backed the staff's difficult decision to remove a group of mature cedars of Lebanon to reveal the great grass amphitheatre. I can remember him saying that if anyone had to explain it on television it would be him.

With Graham Thomas's help a great deal was achieved between 1975 and 1980. While there was little disagreement on fundamentals, Graham was inclined to a less purist view of the restoration, preferring for example to keep a representation of later planting, and he had a weakness for the attractive silver birch that had seeded in from the surrounding commons. With a characteristic pursing of the lips he would say, according to Peter Mansfield, 'I suppose you will have your way because you control the chainsaw.'

One time or another Graham Thomas advised at about one third of the Trust's present collection of gardens, on his own, working only for nine months of the year. Understandably he did not become involved with the many gardens acquired after 1973 when I succeeded him. But there were several more which, although owned by the Trust, for various reasons came under the advisory umbrella proper only later. Many of these were minor gardens where advisory time could not be spared until there were more advisers.

Many more, where he was never involved, were important places where the onerous responsibility for day-to-day management was passed over partly or completely in the 1970s and 1980s by the donor family or tenant, for instance Antony, Nostell, Nymans and Petworth. Speke Hall, Washington Old Hall, Osterley and Ham House have been taken back into National Trust management from local authority control and important gardens such as Chartwell, Scotney, Rowallane and Tatton Park which were advised separately, mainly by Lanning Roper until his sad death in 1983, came into the fold thereafter.

Apart from Attingham and Cliveden, where park management ran with the garden, Graham Thomas was not involved, at any rate officially, with the fifty or so landscape parks owned by the Trust. He would however offer sometimes gratuitous but always constructive suggestions, which were usually accepted, for designed parkland adjacent to drives as at Hardwick Hall or Lyme Park, or to improve shelter or views from the garden as at Killerton, Shugborough and Farnborough Hall. As with his advice in gardens, all this preceded combined historic surveys and research of gardens and parks, not to mention conservation and management plans, both of which the gardens advisers pioneered in the late 1970s. Nevertheless these were timely interventions, often in parks where little had been done for decades and on the whole they proved well founded, if sometimes a little rich in exotic species. Nowadays advice and management are based on carefully considered 'Statements of Significance' which should encapsulate the relative importance of the property in terms of all its qualities, including its history and horticulture.

Some gardens stand out as Graham Thomas's great achievements in conservation (including renovation and a degree of restoration, adaptation and reworking, which are indivisible from the process). Comprehensive restoration of semi-derelict sites is easier as well as always second best to continuous conservation and renewal, because inevitably much is lost when totally replacing derelict features. The precious thread of continuity is always broken.

In long-term conservation great skill and judgement is needed to decide priority for progressive felling, pruning, clearance, reconstruction and replanting, especially where resources are stretched and any apparent change is unwelcome among those who live there or know the garden well. Graham Thomas was usually adept at striking the right balance between boldness and caution, always with a long-term goal in mind, persistently pursued. This kind of continuing care and consistent renewal is the primary purpose of the Trust.

Such was the case at Mount Stewart, one of the Trust's greatest gardens of fifty acres in extent. In the scope of its features, the individuality of its design, the quality and variety of its plant collection and the significance of its family and their connections it is unsurpassed. In 1970 in the words of Nigel Marshall, 'It was not totally neglected but had become rather tired.' Trees were overgrown, many features were overshadowed and had lost their defining qualities; statuary and hard features were crumbling.

Unreliable under clipping, *Cupressus macrocarpa* hedges were replaced with yew and x *Cupressocyparis leylandii.* The Italian Garden, Spanish Garden and Sunken Garden parterres were replanted and much of the Lily Wood and the extensive pleasure ground around the lake renovated so as to restore a balance between the spacious glades and the luxuriant planting that typifies Mount Stewart. The already diverse plant collection was further enriched, especially with southern hemisphere plants, and the wide range of tender rhododendrons assembled by Lady Londonderry were identified, propagated and augmented. All the while Thomas was badgering everyone for funds to restore the importantly symbolic statuary and the structure of paving and steps, a process that was completed only after he finally retired in 1985. These things are never finished.

Graham Thomas advised at Cliveden for more than twenty-five years, longer than anywhere else; time enough to transform the garden, which he did in partnership with Philip Cotton and Christopher Wall. Occupying a magnificent site overlooking the Thames, it embodies features accumulated over more than three centuries. With its extensive avenues, woodland and parkland, it is huge and its connection with a series of distinguished owners, including the Astor family, adds to its significance.

In 1942 Waldorf Astor gave the property to the Trust and it granted a lease back to the family in the person of Lord (Bill) Astor. Then on his third wife, he lived there and managed the gardeners with funds from a charitable trust until the late 1960s. Michael Rogers, area agent for the region, recalls being 'summoned to Cliveden' in the late 1950s and proposing a visit 'by our expert gardens adviser Graham Thomas'. 'Bill Astor ... a large, affable but eccentric man ... appeared in a flowing cloak and a Tyrolean hat. We toured the garden, he avoiding the old parts (... too many new plantings to the detriment of the older and more important areas), concentrating on his plans and we trying to divert him to the old parts. It was difficult. We lunched in the panelled dining room ... waited on by servants in livery. The drink flowed but Graham drank only orange juice. Lord Astor asked if we played croquet. Stupidly I said yes. He summoned the butler – "coffee on the croquet lawn". Would I partner Graham and would we start? I lined up my ball for the first hoop ... The ball shot forward through the first hoop, straight up the long side and through the next one. Silence. "You've played before." To me it seemed a miracle. After that we did very badly. We departed having achieved nothing.' Such were the hazards of being a gardens adviser.

But by the time Thomas finally retired all areas were 'presentable' and the property had become one of the most popular in the Trust, with all the challenges that status brings. Beginning with the great parterre and its surrounding lime trees, each separate feature was renovated in turn – Ilex Grove, Rose Garden, Long Garden, Japanese Garden, where he artfully screened the adjoining car park and for which he provided many plants from his own garden – 'Graham [arriving] at the wheel of his estate car completely surrounded by clumps of plants.' His two main innovations were the giant Jekyll-style herbaceous borders either side of the front court and an arrangement of shrubs in pink and purple at the east end of the house.

Sheffield Park was a favourite of Graham and another garden at which I asked him to continue advising until the early 1980s, finishing mercifully before the great storm of 1986. A close and consistent partnership between head gardener and adviser is important in achieving the maximum in any garden and here Archie Skinner quickly became a committed disciple after his appointment in 1972. Prompting one another, they carried out a great deal of specimen tree and shrub planting to augment the great autumn display. They also developed marginal plantings of herbaceous plants around the lakes and created a stream garden from scratch. Undoubtedly their greatest achievement was the extension of access around the third lake, which gave the garden a whole new dimension, together with the associated clearances and plantings involved in this ambitious exercise.

Graham knew how to put someone down. Archie Skinner recounts an incident in the shop 'when a lady, looking at cheap, small, soft-backed gardening books on a turntable (recognizing Graham) said, "Mr Thomas why don't you write books like this, they sell ever so well?" to which he replied, "Madam, I do not write books to sell. I write books because I have something to say. Good morning." '

Graham's only serious gardening in Northumberland was at Wallington. Energetically encouraged by the regional agent Ben Proud, he formed a highly effective partnership with head gardener Geoffrey Moon from 1958 for seventeen years until I took over in the mid-1970s. Geoffrey relates how the six-acre walled garden 'had suffered during the war' and was used as a market garden, 'growing strawberries, raspberries and blackcurrants and chrysanths outdoors with bedding plants, tomatoes and cucumbers in the glasshouses' until 1960.

In little more than ten years they virtually redesigned, reconstructed and replanted the whole layout, to create a fascinating flower garden of great charm and interest, now much cherished in the area and in the Trust generally. Reduced to a maximum of five gardeners to cover the five acres of pleasure ground around the Hall, thirty acres of garden woodland and the walled garden, economy of labour was the ruling principle; nor was there much money. With the conservative and ever-watchful donor family in residence it is remarkable how much radical change was achieved in a decade. Borders were cleaned of perennial weeds and replanted in Graham Thomas's highly sophisticated Jekyll style – 'a bit of Surrey in Northumberland' as someone unkindly remarked. The open 'cundy' or conduit running through the garden was converted into a rocky stream furnished with plants.

The conservatory, now one of the best-loved in the Trust, was refurbished, replanted and reopened and its propagating houses, which also supply plants for the Hall, were repaired. On the other hand derelict greenhouses, beyond repair, in the lower part of the walled garden were demolished and replaced with a relaxed, informal area of grass and bulbs with trees and shrubs of bold foliage. At the lowest point is a plastic-lined fish pond which had a few adventures in the early years when the cundy, here running under the pool, became blocked, the head of water causing a blowout; hence a 'barrage balloon' instead of a pond. Eventually a bypass for the stream overcame the problem.

Although magnificent in its site and design, remarkable in its range and diversity and unmatched in its historical significance, the garden at Powis had become run down because of a passive and complacent regime and a shortage of funds. The appointment of Jimmy Hancock in 1972 was the catalyst for a transformation. A man of immense commitment and energy, he brought with him high horticultural skills and a passion for propagating plants. Although it was never a comfortable relationship the creative tension was highly productive, Jimmy learning a great deal from Graham's advice without ever really admitting it. Perhaps Graham's economical and highly prescriptive approach did not entirely suit Jimmy's need to discuss everything at length and be identified personally with every change.

An enormous amount was achieved in little more than a decade, including the renovation of hedges and topiary, the planting of tender rhododendrons in the Aviary, clearance and replanting in the Wilderness and the addition of many shrubs and climbers. Undoubtedly the greatest step forward was the replanting of the great double borders on the Orangery Terrace and the Autumn Border on the Apple Slope Terrace. Full of 'country house' perennial weeds, they had to be thoroughly cleaned and manured before Graham's great designs could be attempted, involving the accumulation of many herbaceous plants and coinciding with the publication of *Perennial Garden Plants* (1976). Because the rich, well-manured soil did not suit everything, several have been moved or substituted but that is the way of borders, which cannot and should not remain static. Nevertheless these borders still constitute a masterpiece of Graham Thomas's sophisticated Jekyll style, using an astonishing range of plants, imaginatively colour-graded from one end of the Terrace to the other.

Graham always enjoyed his visits to Cornwall, usually staying at one of the big Falmouth hotels, often to include a weekend. On the way he would call at Cotehele, where he renovated the terraces below the house, opened the cut-flower area to visitors and planted many trees, especially in a sloping meadow above the garden, and a now-enormous weeping silver lime, Graham's signature tree.

At Lanhydrock he worked highly effectively for several years with the head gardener Peter Borlase for whom nothing was too difficult. They cleared and pruned the overgrown Victorian rhododendrons in this big garden and diversified the range of plants, widening the period of display and beginning to expand the magnolias, now one of the country's greatest collections. Perhaps his most telling and lasting development was the doubling of the size of the herbaceous garden from being a half-circle into a full circle, thereby adding greatly to summer colour and interest.

Another of his favourite visits was Trelissick, where he had a stimulating and enjoyable relationship with the irrepressible head gardener, Jack Lilley. Although together they carried out a great deal of renovation and replanting, much of this work was undone by the droughts and frosts of the early 1980s and the storms of 1990 and 1991 when many plants died and many trees fell. As well as a ha-ha into the park, his continuing legacy is an area of several acres over the road, called Carcadden, reached by a new bridge. Formerly a derelict orchard, this became an extension of the garden's informal-style pleasure ground, with a wide range of ornamental trees and shrubs, including conifers, magnolias and hydrangeas, which he established as a speciality of the garden as a whole.

Management at Trengwainton remained in the hands of the donor family through Major Simon Bolitho and Graham Thomas's advice was strictly that. In Cornwall, where growth and decay are rapid, gardens need constant adjustment and pruning, sometimes brutal. Fortunately Graham had the presence and the reputation to command respect. Tenants like

Major Bolitho listened even if they did not always do everything that was recommended. At Trengwainton the garden tour would include at least Major Bolitho (and sometimes Mrs Bolitho), the family's agent for the estate (Jimmy Scobie), the Trust's managing agent, the Trust's historic buildings representative, the head gardener (Peter Horder) and the gardens adviser.

Peter Mansfield recalls how 'a long caravan would wind around the garden twice a year and G. would do his best to persuade ... Following a severe storm in December 1979, Simon had decided to create a brand new part of the garden, complete with planting scheme without even consulting the National Trust or even G. ... to be called the "Jubilee Garden" (the Queen's Silver Jubilee was in 1977). G. resembled a goldfish – opening and closing his mouth but quite unable to find a sound which would be appropriate. Admitting defeat ... he would [henceforth] use it as a [ritual] humorous interlude in our perambulations.'

With the droughts and storms of the 1980s and 1990s, much has changed at Killerton since Graham's time. But along with the head gardener Arthur Godfrey he added many plants to widen the range of trees and shrubs and extend the season for display as well as to augment the traditional range of rhododendrons, azaleas and magnolias. His double-sided, Jekyll-style, mainly herbaceous border survives, slightly developed, having given pleasure to countless thousands of visitors over the years. With Michael Trinick, area agent in the 1960s, he provided the garden with a ha-ha linking the lower part of it to the park. Graham Thomas also made a ha-ha to great effect at Saltram to provide an unbroken view into the park from the house and, as he put it, 'to prevent the cattle leaving their offerings at the front door'.

Since 1955 Graham had been advising in Norfolk and Suffolk and had done much to improve standards and develop a positive and progressive approach to upkeep and renewal, especially at places like Blickling, where he planted hedges to enclose the parterre, and Peckover, where he moved a small pool and redesigned and replanted several borders.

Perhaps the most touching example of Graham's ability to inspire improvement is at Oxburgh Hall, a romantic, moated house near Swaffham, set in the fen with eighteen and a half acres around the house, all that remained of a big estate. After war-time neglect, Fred Greef, the extraordinarily devoted gardener, had single-handedly struggled to restore the extensive lawns, a long herbaceous border and 'the French garden', an enormous parterre. This turned out to have been copied in 1845 by Sir Henry Paston-Bedingfeld from a genuine example which appeared in John James's translation of 1712 from A.J. Dezallier d'Argenville's *La Théorie et la Pratique du Jardinage*. Fred Greef had no plan but, given a pad of graph paper, he impressed Graham by reproducing the layout pretty accurately from memory. Thereafter the pattern was made crisper and replanted and the garden was progressively improved thanks to the inspired energy and enthusiasm of the gardener, who always had a written list of questions ready when Graham came.

The important part of any visit by Graham Thomas to Lyme Park, according to Christopher Wall, invariably his companion, was a picnic on the moor which had to include bilberry and cream tarts from a certain shop in nearby Disley. The challenge of Lyme Park was that it was staffed and managed by Stockport Corporation as a public park, with no charge for entry, which made it prone to misuse and casual vandalism. The annual bedding displays were well up to the best public parks practice, which suited this essentially Victorian layout, but it had lost most of the subtleties of a country house garden, trampled or oversimplified into dull expanses of grass separated by overgrown evergreens. Graham quickly established an effective rapport with Geoff Burrows and his colleagues of Stockport Corporation and inspired a programme of progressive renovation and replanting, including the spectacular sunken Dutch Garden, the pruning of laurels and yews and transformation of a barren area of streamside called Killtime, replanting it with herbaceous perennials and late-flowering shrubs. He also redesigned the double herbaceous borders, a scheme which has now been faithfully restored as a tribute to his skill and artistry.

After its decline during and after the war and an unfortunate period of management by Nancy Lindsay, Hidcote was an early preoccupation in Graham Thomas's career with the Trust. Of all the Trust's flower gardens, Hidcote is probably the most important and the most demanding — complex, labour-intensive, fragile — with the least evidence of the maker's motives and intentions. It depends on the one hand on precision with hedges, topiary, edges and lawns and on the other on subtle plantsmanship and colour co-ordinated informality. With head gardener Harry Burrows, Graham Thomas brought Hidcote back from the edge of dereliction to be one of the Trust's prime attractions, with all the problems that mass visiting brings.

The whole garden was reworked and regenerated, with Harry Burrows energetically leading the way with thinning, pruning, hedging and topiary and Graham exploiting the whole range of his plantsmanship, design ability and aesthetic judgement. The relationship was not an easy one — chalk and cheese — but it got results. There was no money and sadly decrepit greenhouse structures had to be removed and some areas simplified, for instance the kitchen garden. Far fewer tender plants were grown in pots and tubs because their overwintering quarters had gone.

It was a huge achievement, with Graham interpreting each area according to what he found and what could be remembered. If he sometimes imposed his own personality it was usually because of a vacuum of knowledge or because of changed circumstances. What matters is that everything was done well, with conviction, much as an enlightened private owner might have done.

At Sissinghurst the situation could not have been more different, although in many respects the two gardens are similar. With Pam Schwerdt and Sibylle Kreutzberger as joint head gardeners the Trust had inherited outstanding talent in every aspect of gardening – craftsmanship, technical understanding, aesthetic sensibility, plantsmanship, foresight, good judgement and managerial ability – as well as people who had worked directly under the garden's creator. Between them they continually honed their own professional expectations to higher and higher standards, bringing the garden and all involved along with them. Sissinghurst, as recreated by Pam and Sibylle, with the organizational backing of the Trust, was arguably the most influential garden of the western world during the 1960s, 1970s and 1980s. Graham Thomas's role there was mainly to support, encourage and protect, while provoking ever-higher standards of plantsmanship and plant association, which he was ideally qualified to do.

Even his greatest admirers would not claim that Graham Thomas was a highly imaginative or innovative designer of gardens. As James Russell once confided, 'originality was not his forte', except in the sensitive way he was able to respond to existing layouts, whether extant or relict. His strength lay in his expertise at enriching, adapting and renovating gardens which had been neglected but more particularly those which may have been 'maintained' but without any creative input or development over the years. This was true as much with his private commissions as with his work with the National Trust. In fact this special skill and sensitive opportunism is rarer than expertise in innovative design, exercising one's ego being easier than suppressing it during the creative process.

He was adept at picking up the spirit of a place and designing a scheme complementary to it. In the late 1960s, before historicist restoration or recreation became obligatory, Graham designed a small garden of great charm for East Riddlesden Hall, which successfully reflected the scale and character of this small seventeenth-century manor house while making best use of the site to grow an attractive arrangement of interesting plants, fruit and herbs.

Undoubtedly the garden by which he will be best remembered is Mottisfont, where he created a renowned rose garden, beginning just after I joined the National Trust in the early 1970s. Having, with the Royal National Rose Society, assembled an unrivalled collection of mostly pre-1900 roses, Graham was looking for a permanent home for them. When Mrs Russell gave up her tenancy of the walled garden at Mottisfont the regional agent, Sir Dawson Bates, was highly sympathetic to the idea of developing it as a rose garden and he and Graham persuaded the Trust, despite no long-term funding. Now it is the National Collection of old roses and an annual pilgrimage for many thousands of rose lovers.

Thanks to the walled garden being in good order generally and the soil being in good heart, the roses grew well.

Mottisfont shows Graham Thomas at his best, boldly but sensitively adapting and enriching a conventional kitchen garden layout, retaining its paths and box hedges, dipping pond and occasional old fruit tree while superimposing a heady mixture of climbing and shrub roses, interspersed with complementary herbaceous and ground-covering hardy perennials. Continually refined and further developed in the 1980s and 1990s, Mottisfont is Graham's masterpiece.

The word most often used about Graham Thomas is 'incomparable'. He was a unique phenomenon. But the unexpectedly terse and puzzling comment from Christopher Lloyd was 'monolith' – massive? intractable? uniform? undifferentiated? Thomas pursued his own vision of perfection relentlessly, even ruthlessly, in every aspect of his life. It is a tribute to him that everyone who knew him is proud of that fact and as Martin Drury would say, 'If you have shaken hands with Graham Thomas you have established a direct link with Gertrude Jekyll, whose hand he shook.' In *The English Garden: A Social History* (2001), Charles Quest-Ritson rightly says that he was 'central to this [post-war] renaissance of English Gardening'. He was always generous with his knowledge and time with young people and was an effective mentor, who inspired great loyalty among his acolytes. James Russell, distinguished garden designer and colleague at Sunningdale said, 'Graham always wanted to be tops', and he was.

John Sales
JULY 2003

My thoughts are with the Dead; with them
I live in long-past years,
Their virtues love, their faults condemn,
Partake their hopes and fears;
And from their lessons seek and find
Instruction with an humble mind.

My hopes are with the Dead; anon
My place with them will be,
And I with them shall travel on
Through all Futurity;
Yet leaving here a name, I trust,
That will not perish in the dust.

Robert Southey (1774–1843), *His Books*

OVERTURE

WHEN A FULL HISTORY of gardening and gardeners in the British Isles comes to be written in the distant future, I think the twentieth century will loom large. Not only did it begin in Edwardian prosperity but so many things conspired to make it noteworthy: science gave it a special fillip. The *craft* was developed to the full, both by hand and machine; past history was studied and worked over so that there was little fresh to be considered – apart from outlandish new materials and ideas. Above all it was *the* century when the introduction of innumerable trees, shrubs and plants (having been anticipated in the previous century) added an unimaginable richness to our gardens.

In addition the art of hybridizing plants, first understood in the late 1880s, was given full rein and the possibilities were and are incalculable. (Not always, I may add, to the credit of the Creator's palette and ideas!) Whether it will prove a good thing to have man in charge of the development of plants and animals – and, indeed, mankind – remains to be seen.

Over the centuries we have become used to seeing evergreen shrubs in our gardens. Time was, in Tudor days, when the few native evergreens could be numbered on the fingers of one hand: pine, holly, ivy, box and common privet; but 'greens' – as they were first called – increased abundantly. Many proved hardy, although they were originally grown in 'green' houses for protection as in the main they were brought from warmer climates than ours. Prior to the Ice Age evergreens were growing in what has become known as Europe, but as the ice receded the evergreens were unable to recolonize the land above the belt of the mountains and hills which stretch from western Spain away to the Himalaya. This huge mountainous barrier is almost impossible to visualize. The geologists have found that the top of Mont Blanc is composed of rock from North Africa folded over what has become known as the Mediterranean Sea. And the farther east the mountains are studied, the higher and more impregnable they become. Just the opposite obtains in North America where the chains of mountains run mainly from north to south and thus offered little barrier to the migration of plants from south to north as the temperatures eased.

In order to make this little book appear to cover the twentieth century, I feel it necessary to prepare the way by recalling some of the many famous gardeners of its early years. The first twenty years or so were very exciting for gardeners, in the main because more rapid transport enabled seeds and plants to be brought more quickly from foreign countries to Britain, Holland and France. Enthusiasm for the introduction of new plants had been increasing since the nineteenth century and reached a crescendo around 1900, continuing after the Great War until and after the Second World War. It is unlikely that this wonderful period will ever be equalled from the point of view of new natural varieties from both hemispheres which would be hardy in north Europe. The novelties of the future for our gardens lie mainly in the hands of the plant breeders and selectors.

If we go back to about 1875 we shall still be in the Victorian period when gardening was largely given over to the head gardeners of great estates. With perhaps as many as a hundred assistants some head gardeners became so powerful that greenhouse doors were only opened by their own keys. The

gardening practised was neither an art nor a science but simply
the growing of showy and exotic plants, grouped in spectacular
bedding-out schemes or shelf-by-shelf under cover. It was
William Robinson late in the nineteenth century who first
inveighed against this sort of display, which we should now call
vulgar. The art of gardening came gradually, much as
demonstrated by Heather Muir and Gertrude Jekyll and later
by Lawrence Johnston at Hidcote. His red borders were the
first of such and, like those of Lady Burnett at Crathes, owed
much to what we call 'copper' foliage. And we cannot leave out
of this little group Phyllis Reiss who produced something well
out of the ordinary: a border of scarlet, yellow, and white
flowers offset by grey foliage. It was made one of a pair with
the opposite border in muted tones by the grey foliage. Lady
Londonderry at Mount Stewart, Northern Ireland, was also in
the van of artistic gardening.

It is of course impossible for me to do more than comment
on the designers of gardens during the first quarter of the
century. One important contribution is Reginald Blomfield's
impressive design of a vast formal garden at Mellerstain,
Berwickshire. This is in safe keeping, fortunately. To Lutyens
and Jekyll we owe Heywood, Co. Laois, Eire, Folly Farm,
Berkshire and the spectacular Hestercombe in Somerset where
Lutyens combined with Jekyll in 1917 to give us the splendid
design in front of the house which is now so well maintained.
The little formal garden at Batemans, Sussex, was designed by
Rudyard Kipling. These all date back to the first decade.

One of the many great names of the early years of the
century is H. Avray Tipping, who, among many other essays,
worked at Chequers, Buckinghamshire, and Mounton House,
Monmouthshire. In the north we have to acknowledge many
fine garden designs to T.H. Mawson, whose book *The Art and*

Craft of Garden Making (1900) had a great influence. L. Rome Guthrie has two important gardens still in good order in Townhill Park, Southampton and Chelwood Vachery in Sussex. The flamboyant and gifted Norah Lindsay has left us the great parterre at Blickling Hall, Norfolk, while the intriguing water-parterre at Blenheim Palace, Oxfordshire, designed by Achille Duchêne, 1925–30, only needed its patterns of dwarf box renewing to bring it to its former glory.

To be a gardener in those days usually entailed a long training. Known as 'improvers', young men went from one great garden to another, staying perhaps for two years in each establishment until the skills were all learnt and the tools mastered: digging, hoeing, potting, watering, sweeping, mowing and the like. After some six or eight years they were considered fit to be a foreman or even a head gardener. They lived in bothies on the estates. They were helped by ponies and horses; otherwise it was hand labour all the time. Hand barrows, water barrows, wheelbarrows; cans for watering; knives, followed later by secateurs, for pruning; greenhouses and frames ventilated by hand; sodium chlorate as one of the first aids against weeds, likewise soft soap for use against aphids, applied by hand sprayers fed from a bucket. Furnaces were stoked by hand and I remember as late as 1926 great fire-hot, choking lumps of clinker being dragged out in dreadful conditions.

The head gardeners could be very strict and tiresome. It was considered important in planting, say, wallflowers and geraniums, forget-me-nots or lobelias and calceolarias, not to let more than three plants appear to be in a row, and preferably only two! For beds and borders needing extra rich feeding, double-trenching was the order of the day, with manure put in the bottom of the trench, to come to the top layer the following year. Even as late as 1926 this was still carried on; in fact I spent nearly a whole winter in digging one way or another. It was a craft and was governed much by growth and death, of trees and owners.

It was some time before the old craft and the growing art were joined by a scientific approach, but it could be said that quite early in the twentieth century science began to get a considerable grip on horticulture. This can be measured by the rise of experimental stations. Wye and Swanley Colleges, and Rothamsted, were flourishing during the later part of the previous century. Long Ashton, the John Innes Institute and East Malling followed, with genetics a big subject at the John Innes as well as soils and manures. Waterperry was not opened until 1932, but by then we may say that science had become a necessary part of gardening and brought us huge benefits in pedigree rootstocks, weedkillers, insecticides, fertilizers and machinery. Today the instruction courses in horticulture lean heavily towards science and paperwork and young graduates can hardly be called true gardeners.

Societies for the furtherance of special genera have been formed by enthusiasts from time to time. Over all stands the Royal Horticultural Society which has gone from strength to strength. It now has many thousands of members and adds its great weight and experience to every possible facet of horticulture. It is difficult to see how gardening as a hobby or a livelihood could exist or progress without it. All the great names mentioned in this book would have been members of it during a part of their lives and it derives great strength from this fact. That splendid volume, *The Story of the Royal Horticultural Society, 1804–1968*, should be read or referred to by readers of this little effort. It is by Dr H.R. Fletcher, at one time the Director of Wisley, and was published by the Oxford University Press in 1969.

The New Flora and Silva, published in the 1930s, undertook a survey of somewhat tender shrubs and among the noted growers consulted were the following: A. Harley, Devonhall, Perthshire; E.H.M. Cox, Glendoick, Perthshire; The Marquess of Headfort, Kells, Co. Meath; The Countess Grey, Howick, Northumberland; R.B. Cooke, Kilbryde, Northumberland; H.C. Baker, Oaklands, Bristol; Major A. Pam, Wormley Bury, Hertfordshire. These names, together with those already mentioned, give an indication of the great gardening fraternity who were living in the first quarter of the century. There were of course many others. But it was largely through the efforts and enthusiasm of these great gardeners that gardening progressed towards mid-century, until the present writer was old enough to take up the tale, meeting, as the years passed, many of these personalities.

THE TWENTIETH CENTURY was specially noted for the vast increase in the introduction of foreign plants new to our gardens, especially from eastern Asia, North America and the southern hemisphere. Transport of living material, including live plants, had become much easier. There was a constant flow of professional plant and seed collectors, particularly to western China, Nepal and neighbouring countries. Their names stand out like a peal of bells: Wilson, Forrest and Ward; Rock, Farrer and Purdom; and those of more modern times such as Ludlow, Sherriff, Comber, Sykes, Williams and Potanin, up to the end of the century. Among all the many hardy species brought into cultivation the genus *Rhododendron* stands pre-eminent, with magnolias a close second, followed by conifers, shrubs and plants in general including alpines.

From about 1925 the steady surge of new species, having reached flowering stage, needed reviewing and classifying. But

gardeners, being the keen spirits that they are, did not leave
them as they were. Instead many started hybridizing them with
species already established. This particularly applied to
rhododendrons. New species brought new colours of flowers
and leaves, and new sizes; leaves might be two to three feet long,
or less than an inch, and the plants ranged from a few inches to
twenty-five feet or more. *Rhododendron griersonianum*, *R. facetum*
(syn. *R. eriogynum*) and *R. dichroanthum* gave sharper reds and even
orange to the palette, while pure yellow occurred in *R. wardii*
and *R. cinnabarinum* subsp. *xanthocodon* (including *R. c. subsp. x.*
Concatenans Group, syn. *R. concatenans*). *R. williamsianum*
introduced a neat, low, rounded habit and *R. forrestii* and its
relatives brought scarlet flowers on creeping plants, while the
many dwarf species of the *Saluenense* and *Hippophaeoides* Sections
bear tiny leaves and small flowers, assorting well with plantings
of heathers.

With such a gleaning of rhododendrons to cope with it was
fortunate that the climate in Cornwall, western Scotland and
Ireland approximated to that of parts of eastern Asia. Many
famous gardeners in those areas were able to finance
expeditions. A few that come to mind are Lord Stair, Sir John
Stirling Maxwell, Lord Aberconway, J.B. Stevenson, Colonel
Stephenson Clarke and G.W.E. Loder (later Lord Wakehurst).
Canon H.N. Ellacombe of Bitton, Gloucestershire; Charles
Eley, Suffolk; Lord Headfort of Co. Meath; George Johnstone
of Trewithen, Cornwall; Sir Frank Crisp of Henley-on-
Thames; F.J. Hanbury, East Grinstead – all were to the fore in
the earliest quarter of the century. But enthusiasm for new
plants rode high and Lord Headfort led the way for a
conference on the new conifers; Sir William Lawrence did
likewise for the formation of a Society for Alpine Plants and
Major Stern (later Sir Frederick) agitated for a lily conference.

A.K. Bulley, the owner of Bees' Seeds of Chester, was in the forefront and his garden on the Wirral is now the Liverpool University Botanic Garden. He financed George Forrest on several expeditions. Other great finds of Forrest went to J.C. Williams at Caerhays, Cornwall, and included *Camellia saluenensis* and *Magnolia campbellii* subsp. *mollicomata*. Farrer found *Gentiana farreri*, *Viburnum farreri* (syn. *V. fragrans*), *Mahonia lomariifolia* and *Meconopsis quintuplinervia* among other treasures.

One of the most enterprising of plant enthusiasts of his day was Thomas Hay, the Superintendent of the Central Parks, London. He had arrangements with the rulers of states in India and the Far East to send him (in bamboo-stem pots) dormant, frozen primulas and other plants, and exhibited them at Royal Horticultural Society shows when thawed and in flower. This splendid effort was capped, though, when he displayed hundreds of the new blue poppies and primulas in the London Parks.

Some great books were written. Among them were *The Trees of Great Britain and Ireland* by Dr Augustine Henry and H.J. Elwes, which appeared in seven parts from 1906 to 1913. Earlier Elwes had lent his vast erudition to a magnificent work on lilies. Murray Hornibrook wrote the first book on dwarf and slow-growing conifers. Reginald Farrer's *The English Rock Garden* was written before the First World War but did not appear in print until 1919. W.J. Bean's *Trees and Shrubs* appeared in 1914 and has remained unsurpassed through three editions. George Johnstone of Trewithen, having nursed many magnolias from seeds, gave us the fruits of his work in *Asiatic Magnolias in Cultivation* in 1955. A whole half century had gone by in assessing and classifying these plants.

Among the welter of new plants a few occur to me, such as *Meconopsis betonicifolia* (which I was growing in my father's garden in Cambridge in 1927) and other blue poppies, *Davidia*, *Rosa moyesii* and *R. xanthina* f. *hugonis*, *Viburnum davidii*, the Kurume azaleas, *Lilium regale*, *Gentiana sino-ornata*, *Salvia pratensis* Haematodes Group, *Thalictrum delavayi* and the snake-bark maples. Last but not least is the Dawn redwood (*Metasequoia glyptostroboides*), a supposed fossil which was found living in China in 1945.

In the early half of the century the Chelsea Show was dominated by famous seedsmen: Sutton's, Carter's and Webb's. Their huge illustrated catalogues were eagerly awaited by the great head gardeners and superintendents of parks, and the business accruing warranted the erection of mountainous exhibits with thousands of showy plants: salpiglossis, antirrhinums, calceolarias, gloxinias, *Primula malacoides* and others, attended by cascades of blue lobelias. Sweet peas (in fortunate years), carnations, clematis and other popular flowers jostled for space. Gradually shrubs became more and more popular from such famous nurseries as Waterer's, Hillier's, Jackman's, Notcutt's, Knap Hill and others. As the century proceeded to half-time other specialists came forward. I shall never forget the exquisite water plant exhibits from Amos Perry of Enfield, who had started his nursery in 1899, nor the peonies from Kelway's of Langport.

In Worcestershire Ernest Ballard did wonders in breeding brighter and larger Michaelmas daisies. (It is worth recalling here that he brought back from its native haunts a lump of rock which had fallen from inaccessible heights and on which were growing quite a dozen *Jancaea heldreichii*.) There were also the amazing results of George Russell's selections of lupins (started in 1912), Blackmore and Langdon's superlative delphiniums and Allwood's carnations.

But horticulture has never stood still. Recent years have seen great advances in the breeding of petunias and busy lizzies. The petunias have gained a prolificity never imagined; unfortunately the busy lizzies, which achieved similar brilliance, have been spoiled by being doubled. Daylilies, which were only seen occasionally, are now available in almost uncountable numbers in the United States and in unimagined colours. The leaves of hostas are a study on their own.

Irises, mainly of the large-flowered Bearded Group, have also their devotees. The enthusiasm for breeding began in Europe and spread to Britain and eventually to the United States. The chosen cultivars have been through several popular phases. It started with the new velvety falls and smoky colours in France and England, went on through brighter colours and larger flowers with Sir Arthur Hort, Sir Michael Foster and W.R. Dykes, then to the United States where the flared falls, the frilling and goffering have reached such a pitch that the original shape of an iris (so captivating) is forgotten. And I see evidence that the selections of the Siberian irises and other groups are going the same way – just as the Japanese breeders did with their own species two hundred years ago.

It is not surprising that the darling flower of all, the rose, has also been touched with progress. Apart from the several species which have been used, the breeding of roses, when it became understood late in the nineteenth century, remained static. The hybrid tea was the ideal rose; it had developed a new impeccable shape in the genus, and so it remained through the first half of the twentieth century. But David C.H. Austin of Wolverhampton, a farmer and the son of a farmer, having been infected with enthusiasm for the old French roses which I had been collecting, decided he would alter the shapes and colours of the favourites and bring in again the soft tones, rich fragrances and fully double array of petals of the old roses. And well has he achieved his aim, so that a number of already established rose-breeders have followed suit. A new garden rose of today is almost bound to have a good array of petals, and moreover very often much greater vigour, depending on the climate where it grows. My own namesake, bred by David, achieves ten feet in California and New Zealand and may often be seen up to five or six feet in this country. As it is no longer the fashion to have sunken or patterned gardens solely for roses, increased interest is being taken in these plants (which after all started life as shrubs, not as bedding plants) for use with other shrubs and plants. An avenue which the breeders have so far neglected is roses for shade; they might well be achieved by the inclusion of the old so-called Ayrshire roses in their stud books; likewise to breed out prickly growths. Instead they have launched so-called 'ground cover roses', though who would want the job of weeding prickly roses in their early years? It is surely a role much better undertaken by low-growing perennials and non-prickly shrubs.

The nurserymen were not idle. Anthony Waterer at Knap Hill Nursery did much for hardy azaleas, which had earlier been bred in Ghent; Lionel de Rothschild followed at Exbury. Thanks to Harold Hillier's great energy and knowledge, Hillier's nursery carried without rival the most exhaustive collection of new and old trees and shrubs in the world. Sweet peas were much improved in size and appeal, but lost most of their scent from 1900 onwards. A very important wholly white daffodil, 'Beersheba', was bred by Engleheart in 1923. Alpine plants and rock gardens came to great strength through the efforts of Clarence Elliott, and W.E.Th. Ingwersen, who had worked some years at Wisley, started his own Birch Farm Nursery in Sussex in 1925.

The first glimmerings of rock gardens occurred with a leaning towards grottoes in the nineteenth century. In the second and third quarters of the twentieth century the rock gardens exhibited at the Chelsea Show reached a very high note. The artistry in the placing of the rocks, accompanied by gushing streams and pools, has never been surpassed, and the planting was usually good also. And yet only one of the fairly regular exhibitors placed the great pieces of beautiful rock as they would be found in nature; the expert who knew about geology, so placing his efforts above all others, was Captain B.H.B. Symons-Jeune. It was not only the attractive rock which was beautifully placed here and there with a pronounced slant into the raised soil to conserve moisture, but the underlying structure, hidden from sight, that was suggested.

In the early part of the century one of the most influential of nurserymen in the pursuit of alpine plants and rock gardens was Backhouse of York. It seems very extraordinary to me how the famous Miss Willmott, at the end of the nineteenth century, should commission a nurseryman from so far north to make for her in Essex a large rocky dell of a northern rock, millstone grit, with no special quality to recommend it except that it was part and parcel of Backhouse's work. The rocks are still in place in her desolate garden; they are angular, not porous (to conserve moisture), nor beautiful. It may be that she had never seen the attractive limestone from Somerset or Westmorland. These two counties supplied most of the favourite rock for exhibits at Chelsea Show and thereafter in our gardens. When it was realized how our landscapes were being denuded in this way, something of an embargo was placed on its sale and transport to the rest of England.

William Wood and Son of Taplow, Buckinghamshire, and George G. Whitelegg of Chislehurst, Kent, were two of the most regular exhibitors on the rock garden bank at Chelsea. They remain in the memory with sheer delight. Another very noted firm, Pulham and Son of Bishop's Stortford,

Hertfordshire, used various stones; some of their work remains at the top western end of the rock garden at Wisley. But their fame was mainly concerned with the grottoesque use of faked stone made on the spot, as at Sandringham. There are some records and photographs of their unique work in my book *The Rock Garden and its Plants*, recording their consummate artistry early in the century. A further great effort was at Friar Park, Henley-on-Thames, where Sir Frank Crisp had an enormous rock garden built of 7,000 tons of rock from Yorkshire with a simulated Matterhorn on top!

One exhibitor struck out all on his own: this was Gavin Jones of Letchworth, Hertfordshire. He, perhaps true to his up-bringing, used Welsh granite and Forest of Dean sandstone, of severe line but magnificent. The brown Hornton (Oxfordshire) rock came later to the fore with some exhibitors, while one firm from the north used astonishing informal and colourful rock which was the leftover from furnaces. Meanwhile various stones had been used in the rock gardens of our botanic gardens – Hornton sandstone at Cambridge, millstone grit and granite at Edinburgh, and a succession of different rocks at Kew. There the atmosphere in the early part of the century caused Westmorland and Derbyshire limestone to turn to near white, and thus Sussex sandstone was used when the rock garden was progressively refashioned by G.H. Preston; it has also been greatly used at Wisley. This stone was also always favoured by Walter Ingwersen's Sussex firm owing partly to proximity, but also because it held several times its own weight in water. But I think the fashion for grandiose rock gardens has been on the wane for a decade or more. Cartage is costly, gardens are smaller, and the cultivation of alpines is leaning towards raised beds with underground watering devices and the alpine house. At Kew elaborate systems to imitate frozen subsoil have been invented.

So LET US NOW leave these preliminary musings and attend to the main list of great gardeners and their gardens, mostly started and all completed during the lifetime of the owners and makers. It is after all the *raison d'être* of the book. I have arranged the book alphabetically under the names of the creators, many of whom were friends of mine, and I learnt much from them. None of us lives long enough to record happenings of a whole century, but in order that this book shall cover as many years as possible, I have recalled in earlier pages many great gardeners that I used to hear about in my young days. Together with these the eminent men and women who created memorable gardens in the last three quarters of the century, now to be briefly recorded, make an impressive assembly. Even so I feel the list is incomplete; other writers would have been able to add other experts.

And just as I was writing the few last words above came the sad news that Her Majesty Queen Elizabeth, The Queen Mother, had died. Patron of the National Trust, the Royal Horticultural Society, the Royal National Rose Society and numerous other charities, she will be remembered for her great love of flowers and gardens. I count myself very fortunate to have lived in her era, though ten years younger. I have been greatly honoured twice by being asked to help with the garden at Royal Lodge in Windsor Great Park; once, when with His Majesty King George VI they were desirous of prolonging the display of the many rhododendrons by adding species and hybrid shrub roses, and later when as the Queen Mother she wished for a small garden of the nineteenth-century roses which she so loved, as I did. She will be much missed and mourned by us all.

THE GATHERING OF THE PLANTS

They come, they come,
The hidden, hallowed promises of spring,
The crocus holds its golden cup to Heaven;
The seeds beneath the loam
Have felt the high sun pierce their covering,
And winter's doom is riven.

Sir William Beach Thomas
The Poems of a Countryman (1945)

THE GARDENERS

Iris missouriensis

THE LORD ABERCONWAY

Bodnant

COLWYN BAY • NORTH WALES

National Trust

MY PEN-FRIEND of long standing, A.T. Johnson (see page 142) wrote asking me to spend a weekend with him and his wife, Nora, in North Wales in the 1930s, adding that 'Bodnant will be open on the Saturday and we could take you there'. Such an invitation was a great opportunity and of course I went. So began a long series of biennial visits only terminated by my friends' deaths.

We had a superb afternoon at Bodnant which confirmed what I had thought from reading about it and seeing exhibits brought all that long way to Chelsea and other shows in London. The second Lord Aberconway had inherited the property; he was also President of the Royal Horticultural Society (RHS) and spared no effort to help the society. At the show in 1929 I had been stunned by the Bodnant exhibit, which contained many rhododendrons of their own raising, *Meconopsis*, primulas, *Arisaema candidissimum*, and other delights.

But to enter Bodnant itself was quite a different matter. Although apparently of mountainous outline, it is only about a hundred feet above sea level, and has at times suffered severely from spring frosts. There was no sign of this on our visit which was in June, when the young summer was at its best. I remember specially *Magnolia sieboldii* subsp. *sinensis* nodding its fragrant white bells over a massed display of *Primula* Asthore hybrids, and great magnolias trained on the several very large retaining walls, for the garden is mainly on a slope with noble planting at every level. It is blessed with a wonderful assortment of well grown plants; I have visited many times and happy memories recall one upper terrace with a large, long border with hundreds of upturned trumpets of glorious blue *Gentiana acaulis*. At another season the pink and crimson water-lilies had for a companion a blue Atlantic cedar; dieramas and lilies, splendid borders of perennials and choice and unusual shrubs, perhaps glimpsed between great tree trunks. Also outcrops of rock, streams and waterfalls, and a spot where the almost unbelievable vermilion of the embothriums strike through every colour. There is a rose terrace under the house and long borders of beautiful shrubs curving away around the slopes. And rhododendrons of every kind, height and colour, including many Bodnant hybrids.

Harry Aberconway exerted a huge influence on the RHS and was the instrument by which Bodnant became one of the leading gardens of the world, an eminence which his son Charles did so much to enhance. They have been aided by three generations of great head gardeners, all named Puddle.

Everywhere you go there is birdsong, the sound of water rushing over the falls, and not least, if you can encourage your eyes to leave the plants and lift, great scenery, perhaps contrasted with reclining sphinxes on a wall.

But it is not a jumble of plants. There is the relief of the canal and long borders set in lawn with the architectural finish of the raised theatre surrounded by big hedges of yew; on the stage is a most splendid seat. At the other end of the canal is the beautiful architectural finish of the little Pin Mill, brought from Gloucestershire.

It is not a static garden; well-run gardens never are. Each time I have been there over some twenty-five years I have found something new and lovely has been achieved. It is truly a feast for the eyes whichever way you look and the huge collection of plants provides the embroidery.

CUTHBERT H.D. ACLAND

Stagshaw
AMBLESIDE • CUMBERLAND
National Trust

CUTHBERT ACLAND HAD BEEN KNOWN as 'Cubby' since boyhood and the abbreviation stuck to him for his whole life. A man of widespread interests and abilities, he decided on forestry as a career and entered the services of the National Trust, first being posted as agent for Polesden Lacey in Surrey. He had been brought up on the Killerton estate in Devon and so had trees as his companions; although in a limy area the arboretum at Killerton is on a small eminence of lime-free soil and so rhododendrons and conifers were, so to speak, in his blood. He must have disliked intensely the chalky escarpment at Polesden, though strangely on that part of the North Downs there are frequent patches of lime-free soil on the hilltops; at Polesden there are actually rhododendrons and sweet chestnuts of considerable size.

Cubby was duly posted to the Lake District. He was given a small house at Stagshaw near Ambleside, with views through the scattered woodland on the hillsides to Lake Windermere. There I met him and a fruitful and delightful friendship ensued over some twenty years. He was on fire to create something in the image of Killerton. Would I help him? Of course, especially as I already had National Trust gardens to attend to in the district. His first action was to thin the woodland above and around his house, and after that to start a planting scheme of all sorts of shrubs and trees, plants and bulbs to give him year-round delight. The land included some rocky outcrops and a small gushing stream. It was made for gardening, and he set about it with a will. I always stayed with him for a night or two when my work took me to his district, and usually his first request was, 'What shall I plant *there* to look beautiful *now*?' He had an able-bodied man to help him and never did a year go by without a new planting taking place. I think his deepest love was for rhododendrons and he amassed a considerable collection, grouped according to colour and season, which, though few gardeners realize the fact, extends from November to July and August.

But he included other shrubs, *Styrax*, *Viburnum*, *Magnolia*, *Cornus* and *Eucryphia*, among these. One year I took from my garden a turf-like wad of *Maianthemum bifolium* and another of *Cornus canadensis*. I have often wondered whether they have run all over the slopes, and likewise whether *Rhododendron* 'Fragrantissimum' has survived the winters, protected as it was on rising ground by a rocky outcrop. Wherever the soil was deep enough he continued planting shrubs and bulbs: *Narcissus*, *Camassia*, snowdrops and crocuses.

Almost alone among gardeners he created a moss garden; it was in a little grove of trees and bushes. He collected from around the district every moss he could find, identified them and got them to grow. In addition his sense of humour inspired him to make what he called moss-balls. These were composed of lumps of *Leucobryum glaucum* tied into balls and kicked around as one passed!

There was a large old garden next door completely neglected and overrun by native weeds, but also by *Rubus spectabilis*, the salmonberry, whose raspberry-like fruits make a delicious dish in August with cream and sugar. It is a rampant spreader and hails from western North America. To crown all in this entrancing lakeland spot was an old wall where it amazed me to find haberleas were seeding themselves. But of course we were trespassing.

Cubby spent something like twenty years creating beauty for the future and well did he do it. His last year or so was clouded by illness. I had retired from the northern properties but eventually heard he was in a hospital in Hertfordshire. I immediately set out to visit him. It was a day in February after a spell of mild weather and so I picked a few heads of early rhododendrons for him. I arrived by train at about twelve noon. But the Sister informed me that he had died, peacefully, that very morning. I felt deeply saddened and bereft and left the flowers with her to cheer the ward.

THE AMORYS

Knightshayes Court
TIVERTON • DEVON
National Trust

SIR JOHN AND LADY HEATHCOAT-AMORY must have been early risers; they had a London house and were sure to arrive at the Chelsea Show soon after it had opened. And so they used to come to our exhibit before the crowds and always found something they wished to order. This was in the early 1950s. Lady Amory had been Joyce Wethered, the famous golfer, and one of the first things they did was to make a little series of putting greens below the house and garden. But I fancy that coming to Knightshayes and getting to know Mrs Ludovic Amory (Sir John's aunt), who lived only a few miles away and was an expert gardener, turned her head towards gardening. She could not have been in a more suitable place for it.

It happened that my friend Gwendolyn Anley (see page 70) was a distant relative of Mrs Amory and had long wanted to visit her. Their common ancestor was Sir Joshua Rowley, whose three-pronged silver forks Gwenda and I used when at Glyndebourne. The result of all this was that at the next Chelsea Show I was asked whether I would bring Gwenda down for a weekend. It was eventually fixed for early May in the following year.

We arrived at Tiverton on time and went through the big gates to enter an informal avenue of great trees, including immense Cornish elms and huge Turkey oaks. Suddenly the

Gentiana asclepiadea 'Knightshayes' (top) and other forms

house came into view: a great Victorian pile of warm-coloured stone on an eminence. I think we both gasped in astonishment.

We went through the great hall and entered the library where we were welcomed with warmth. After lunch we started a tour of the garden which was undoubtedly looking at its spring best. I found it difficult to tear myself away from the superb view down the park, over the formal garden set with great clipped yews, and indeed from the walls of the Court where so many choice things grew. A flight of steps led to the alpine borders supported by retaining walls and formal hedged gardens to the new garden beyond. This was the pride and joy of the owners. Much if not all of the preparatory work and planting had been done by Jack and Joyce. Scattered trees made the conditions right for rhododendrons, maples and woodland shrubs of all kinds. There was something new and unique at every turning point and the whole area was dominated by some large variegated *Aralia chinensis* with stretches of primulas, shortias, ferns, trilliums, cypripediums and several species of *Meconopsis*.

We lingered long over all the treasures, returning to the Court by way of the hedged formal gardens whose banks and environments were decorated by further joys. One formal garden had some nondescript beds in it. Jack subsequently purchased an ancient lead tank and asked me to produce a new plan for the garden, which I did. The colours are kept cool in order not to detract from the lead tank.

On the Sunday we were taken to Mrs Amory's garden. This had been cleverly designed in terraces and was bounded on two sides by a rushing stream. There was an astonishing assembly of lovely plants, including stretch after stretch of the double, pure white pheasant's eye *Narcissus poeticus* 'Plenus'. This was a revelation; it has never flowered for me with any enjoyment in dry Surrey. The garden was in impeccable order. And of course

Sir Joshua Rowley's name was quoted freely. The terraced borders under the house contain many roses and sun-loving shrubs and plants but these were absorbed on later visits.

This was only the first visit. I was shortly to take up advisory work for the National Trust at nearby Killerton and Cotehele, and was bidden to come and stay whenever in the district. And what lovely visits they were! The walk round the ever enlarging garden was always full of interest, followed by a giant loudspeaker in the vast drawing room of an evening, playing magnificent music.

The garden was enlarged by several acres, eating into the larch wood. Jack was all for a collection of shrubs; *Rhododendron augustinii* made a haze of lavender blue next to some pale yellows, while elsewhere all sorts of rarities were to be seen: *Euonymus tingens*, *Acradenia frankliniae*, *Acer pensylvanicum* 'Erythrocladum' for its colourful twigs in winter, unusual conifers – the list seems endless. Joyce on the other hand, much as she had also been smitten with the beauty of shrubs, magnolias, *Nothofagus* – in fact everything – was the expert who raised hardy cyclamens of all kinds, which were distributed in sheets and drifts in the woodland areas. Not only are they a wonderful sight when seen in flower in their thousands but the foliage of many is beautifully marbled.

On the other side (west) of the Court Jack's predecessors had made use of a little stream, damming it to make a pool, and had planted swathes of Ghent hybrid azaleas. To these Joyce added another enthusiasm, after seeing beds of young willows in a nursery; they were so appropriate to the site and gave, being coppiced, a variety of tints in all seasons of the year.

I feel I must quote the last paragraph from my account of the garden in my *Gardens of the National Trust* (1979):

Soon after embarking on this extensive garden making and planting, the Amorys thought it might help to enthuse their old head gardener to pay a visit to Chelsea Show. On the morrow Lady Amory asked whether he had enjoyed his visit and whether he had noted any special plants which might be added to the garden. The reply came: 'No, m'Lady, I don't think there's anything there which we need bother about.' It was an answer that could be interpreted in various ways, but there was no doubt about his own impression of Knightshayes garden.

In due course the whole estate was given to the National Trust. It was a marvellous bequest because all their hard work and imagination was preserved. After Jack's death a series of rooms at the east end of the Court was made suitable for Joyce, who for many years still loved and enjoyed the garden. The National Trust have restored the great rooms to the high Victorian style which had been theirs. It was all a wonderful transformation and I believe is an eye-opener to the public as to just how grand Victorian tastes were.

GWENDOLYN ANLEY

St George's
WOKING • SURREY

GWENDOLYN=ANLEY (this was how she always signed herself)
presided over and worked in a well-designed garden for about
forty years, devoting her considerable energy and skill to the
welfare of a great assembly of plants. For much of the time
she had the help of a full-time gardener, who in turn had the
help of a lad, who eventually became the only garden staff.
Brigadier General Barnett L. Anley did nothing to speak of in
the garden until he retired, and then he took up growing hardy
border carnations.

I think the garden had been laid out, if not designed, by a
landscape firm. It had all the recognized different
compartments: a short drive with a Rambler rose screen and
espalier apples on one side; on the other side beds and a lawn
with fine trees and a tennis court. The levelling of this area
resulted in a cool shady retaining wall at one corner with
supporting walls opposite, flagged path and a herbaceous
border backed by cypresses. Around the house were paved
terraces, more trees in grass, a rock garden, a vegetable garden
with cordon fruit trees, a pergola, and more beds. Then there
was within easy reach of the back door a garage, potting
shed, alpine house, lath houses, and beds of irises. Later a
further strip of garden was acquired; it ran the length of the
ground and was given to ornamental trees and shrubs – in all

perhaps two and a half acres. It was all laid out on a slight eminence on very sandy soil, known locally as Bagshot Sand but without the inhibiting iron 'pan' of many lower areas in the neighbourhood.

Mrs Anley gardened with great skill almost to the end of her life and was always armed with secateurs, raffia, labels and other tools of the trade. I was taken to see her by John Wall, curator of the rock garden at the Royal Horticultural Society's garden at Wisley. Alpines and rock gardens were their keenest interests, as they were, at that time, one of mine. It was somewhat daunting to read a notice on the front gate: 'Considerate people will shut this gate; others are requested to do so.' The notice was mainly because of her pet dog, a Peke, of which over the years she had several. It was a very good notice and had the desired result, but my feelings were somewhat perturbed by another notice over the fireplace in the study: 'If you have nothing to do, please don't do it here.' I need not have worried, however; we were welcomed with great kindness and a long subsequent friendship confirmed that she lavished kindness and consideration on all her friends. The notice merely intimated that – in spite of house and garden staff – she lived a very busy life. She took immense trouble to see that her plants were in the best of health and attributed much to the beneficence of leafmould of which there was always an ample supply available from well-constructed bins. There was no doubt that her outlook was soundly practical, though tempered by a deep appreciation of beauty. Indoors she was preparing her book *Alpine House Culture for Amateurs*; it appeared in 1938 and remained a standard work for a long time.

As the years passed Mrs Anley's interests varied and her energies became concentrated on her new plantings of shrubs, snowdrops (of which she amassed about forty kinds in the 1950s), peonies, including some of the Saunders hybrids from New York, sent over by Miss Sylvia Saunders who was an old friend, and of course irises, of which she maintained a large collection of the most up-to-date of the Bearded Group. These were I think her first and last love. I remember her on almost all fours replanting different sections of the beds in the hottest of summer weather. At the end of one of these beds was a large group of self-sowing *Tulipa whittallii* (now correctly *T. orphanidea* Whittallii Group), which made a splendid display in spring. It was her wide-ranging enthusiasm that made a visit so interesting and also kept her occupied from snowdrop time until autumn, when *Campsis grandiflora* made a spectacular display on the dovecote.

A collection of *Iris* species was gradually accumulated after the war, a job most carefully done in preparation for her second book, *Irises, Their Cultivation and Selection*. Like her former book it was prepared with great care and expertise, and I had the honour of doing some drawings for it. A revised edition was brought out in 1948.

But we must go back to the late 1930s, when Mrs Anley made a trip to Japan. She went with the idea of seeing Japanese gardens and of absorbing Japanese methods with alpines, but came back with a treasury of Japanese thoughts which altered her outlook in many ways. The growing of dwarf conifers had always been one of her enthusiasms; a considerable collection was maintained at one time, and as they were pot-grown she was able to exhibit them at one of the post-war Chelsea Shows. They covered a large table and gained a high award. To them she added imported specimens of bonsai, and started growing her own, under specially constructed lath shelters. I think it was the discipline and economy of cultivating these characterful

LEFT TO RIGHT: *Galanthus nivalis* 'Plenus', G. 'Magnet' G. *caucasicus*; G. *nivalis* 'Straffan', G. *n.* 'Scharlockii'

pieces that proved the great attraction. But the Japanese economy of line was also apparent indoors, where there was often a single shapely branch of shrub or tree placed on table or mantelpiece for appraisal. Japanese prints replaced Crimea War scenes on the walls, and all her skills were brought to bear on thinning and shaping the trees and shrubs in her garden. No tree received more care than *Pyrus salicifolia* 'Pendula'. From an overcrowded huddle of drooping branches it became a sheer masterpiece of elegance.

Hostas became an enthusiasm, fired partly by her visit to Japan, and these and hardy orchids grew well among the shrubs. Shrubs were taken to heart with the assistance of Walter Bentley, a famous gardener at Newbury, Berkshire, and Hugh Armytage-Moore of Rowallane, Co. Down, Northern Ireland (see page 76). They both specialized in the best shrubs and trees. Sir Cedric Morris brought other enthusiasms forward.

The lawns sloped down from the house on all sides except by the garage, which had on its west wall the delectable fig 'White Marseilles', than which none melted faster in my mouth. A lovely young specimen, already white-barked, of *Betula papyrifera* grew near to a blue cedar; Rose 'Mermaid' flowered well on the north of the house until a severe winter killed it to ground level. It survived and grew again. In the shady corner by the tennis court grew a huge clump of *Hepatica* x *media* 'Ballardii' and various ramondas and haberleas, but as a general rule it was a sunny garden and *Pulsatilla vulgaris* seeded itself with abandon. Alas, this did not apply to the forget-me-not-blue 'Budapest' form, of which there was a good clump, a present from Hew Dalrymple, famous for the Bartley strain of primulas.

I am sure Mrs Anley was innately a happy person, despite three great sadnesses – the death of her only daughter at an early age and the loss of her god-daughter, and of her husband later on. She also had the misfortune of watching her garden being invaded by *Equisetum* or mare's-tail. Her house looked over a field owned by Jackman's nursery. Rowland Jackman told me that in an effort to get rid of the weed he had the field scarified every month for two years, but it made no difference. It is known that the roots go down at least sixteen feet. The weed gradually spread over the borders at St George's, went under the house and proceeded to engulf the tennis court and in fact the whole place. It was this gradual disaster that drove her away from the main garden to the areas around the potting shed and alpine house where everything was in pots and containers of one sort or another.

Apart from many visits to her garden at all times of the year, where I knew that a warm welcome awaited me, some of my happiest memories of Gwenda are of music. We both shared a great love of this, and in the 1960s she managed to get four tickets every summer for Glyndebourne, right in the middle of the stalls. While she provided the tickets and supper, I provided the car and we each took a friend. It was a wonderful experience and each evening seemed to be more summery than the last. It was a perfect blending of gardening and music, those two recreations which are so different yet so complementary.

She enriched my life with gifts of several books and much kindness, refuting to the full whatever impression might have been gained by the two notices in early days!

She also enriched our gardens, not only with plants that she so generously gave away, but with plants of her own raising. Many irises were raised but, her usual high standards to the fore, she only named two. One was the splendid dark violet-blue 'Arabi Pasha', which is still to be found in nurseries, and the other 'Mirette', named after her little dog – who would only eat a piece of chocolate if she got down on her knees and gave it to her. This iris is a refined and elegant pale lavender-blue. It is no longer in catalogues, but I still grow it. There were also two plants named after her husband: *Calluna vulgaris* 'Barnett Anley', which is found in many lists today, and a lavender of the same name which seems to have disappeared. Messrs Burkwood and Skipwith of Kingston upon Thames, Surrey, honoured her by naming an *Escallonia* 'Gwendolyn Anley', and this is still grown in many gardens.

HUGH ARMYTAGE-MOORE

Rowallane
SAINTFIELD • CO. DOWN • NORTHERN IRELAND
National Trust

MY FIRST VISIT TO IRELAND was in 1937; it took little persuasion to get me there because I wanted to see Tom Blythe again with whom I had worked at Cambridge. He was a great enthusiast towards shrubs, having worked at Gauntlett's famous nursery at Chiddingfold, Surrey. In addition, he was a nephew of the Smith family who had started the famous Daisy Hill Nursery at Newry, Co. Down. He had returned to a little hamlet near Newry and had stocked a half-acre garden with classic shrubs – some rhododendrons, pierises, eucryphias, hydrangeas, and so forth, and would I go over and make a rock garden for him and spend a few days more to visit Rowallane and go down to Glasnevin at Dublin as well? Of course I would and looked forward to it immensely. We made the rock garden, for which he had plants waiting, and went by rail to Saintfield and thence walked up to Rowallane. I had heard a lot about this famous garden from Tom; how it was on poor soil with sandstone rocks near the surface, where, Mr Moore's uncle had said, 'there was not enough herbage to feed a goat'.

But Hugh thought otherwise and when he inherited the property found there was still good soil in the hollows, though the rocky outcrops were many. Tom and I arrived about ten o'clock on a good morning, rang the bell, and were greeted by a spare figure with trowel, labels and packets of seeds. He took us to three comparatively rare plants, one of which was *Kirengeshoma palmata*, and we knew them all. I heard afterwards that this was his way of finding out whether a visitor was worth taking round the garden! Evidently he thought we were, because he 'had just to go to the potting shed and would be back in a few minutes'. We had a wonderful day with him.

My notebook records seeing *Deutzia purpurascens* and *D. pulchra*, *Actinidia coriacea*, *Berberis calliantha*, *Spiraea trichocarpa*, *Sorbus sargentiana* and many more. But two plants that stay most vividly in my memory are *Cardiocrinum* (*Lilium*) *giganteum* var. *yunnanense* and *Rhododendron campanulatum* subsp. *aeruginosum*. The former was grouped on each side of the path, some five feet high with large rounded leaves and great trumpets of lily flowers in greeny cream with dark red in the throats. My photograph of the plants (in monochrome) has appeared in several publications. A wonderful sight, but perhaps the rhododendron beat it. I had never seen it before; it was not in flower, but the mound of young foliage was at its best – an almost incredible verdigris blue: a sight to remember for a lifetime. I grew it at one time in another garden and when I moved house gave it to Jim Russell to take to Castle Howard.

But perhaps I am going too fast. The walk up the long drive to the house was full of interest. Wherever there was a dell with comparatively deep soil shrubs and trees had been planted during Mr Moore's time, though a few big coniferous trees were planted by his uncle. There was a lovely clearance around the house – which was not notable in any way – with scenic planting of rare conifers and rhododendrons. The drive led to a tower through Irish yews, but we went into the walled garden, originally the kitchen garden, where there were more than enough wonderful shrubs and plants to beguile us until Mr Moore returned. It would be tedious to try to enumerate even half of them, but there were species of rose, magnolias (including a great specimen of *Magnolia* x *watsonii* (*M.* x *wieseneri*), casting its fragrance around, *Viburnum plicatum* f. *tomentosum* 'Rowallane', primulas including 'Rowallane', and farther down the original *Chaenomeles* x *superba* 'Rowallane' and that most splendid of St John's worts, *Hypericum* 'Rowallane'. *Meconopsis betonicifolia* grew well by the arched exit.

By then Mr Moore had rejoined us and took us over to the landscape beyond, carved into areas by old stone walls and planted with a mouth-watering array of carefully placed shrubs and trees and plants, enough to make us feel we were at a transformed Kew. It was wonderful how a man, untrained in horticulture, could have acquired such a remarkable collection of plants of all kinds, conifers included.

I have made many visits in the past and have always come away with renewed admiration for its gentle unassuming beauty, nursed during some fifty years to such a pitch of excellence. Garden visitors are of all sorts and I think I must reinforce this statement by quoting a paragraph from my entry on Rowallane in my book *Gardens of the National Trust*:

Garden visitors can be such a nuisance if the owner is very busy — as Mr Moore undoubtedly was because he designed and planted gardens professionally from time to time, besides working at Rowallane. He once related to me how he dealt with an impossibly bumptious visitor who, no matter what he was shown, always made out that his own specimen was bigger or better. At last, having shown him specimens that he knew were remarkable, Mr Moore said: 'Tell me, do you grow *Hydrangea sargentiana* [now *H. aspera* subsp. *sargentiana*]?' 'Why, yes,' said the visitor, 'I have a fine specimen; it is about 5 feet high and wide and is a magnificent sight, covered with flower heads at the moment.' 'Ah, yes, that's interesting. I was wondering whether it would grow in the crevices of an old brick wall,' said Mr Moore. 'My dear sir,' said the visitor, 'that would be the last place; it likes cool woodland treatment, a sheltered position, and lots of humus in the soil.' His host thanked him, and they moved on past a huge clump of *Philesia buxifolia* and a large bush of *Pseudowintera* (*Drimys*) *colorata* and came later to a shrub whose flowers appear in the middle of what seem to be leaves, which the visitor did not know, *Helwingia japonica*. 'And there', said Mr Moore, 'is my *Hydrangea sargentiana*; I measured it the other day; it is 8 feet high, 14 feet across, and you see it is seeding itself into the brick wall …'

LT.-COL. SIR EDWARD BOLITHO

Trengwainton
PENZANCE • CORNWALL
National Trust

TRENGWAINTON, meaning 'the house of the springs', is a very
old establishment, having a stone arch near the house bearing
the date 1692, but the present house dates from the nineteenth
century. During the twentieth century the remarkable sloping
beds were built in the kitchen garden to provide extra warmth
from the sun, even in that already favoured situation. Greenhouses and frames were also built to help provide enough
vegetables and fruits for the household. This productive area
lies near the main road. The garden as a whole is an odd shape
with a noble sinuous drive leading up to the house which
commands views down to St Michael's Mount. Thus there is
first the original gardened area near the entrance while the
lawns and plants around the house are joined to the great drive
with its stream garden connecting the two. This originally was
in a culvert, but among the many things which Sir Edward did
was to open it to the light and air and plant alongside it
numerous primulas and other moisture-loving plants, so that
flowers went with you all the way up to the house.

It was Sir Edward who, after inheriting the property in
1925, united the three areas by his rich planting of trees and
shrubs. It was a bosky place even in early days, many natives
having been planted over much of the area. Sir Edward

inherited just at the right time to plant the hosts of new trees and shrubs from eastern Asia and elsewhere which were pouring into the country. Fortunately he made friends with three of the important subscribers to the collecting expeditions – J.C. Williams of Caerhays, P.D. Williams of Lanarth and Canon Boscawen at Ludgvan. Sir Edward gave the property to the National Trust in 1961.

It was a great pleasure to me thereafter to be called in to assist with the management of the garden. A succession of

Magnolia x *thompsoniana*

worthy head gardeners had left their mark, but above all Sir Edward knew his plants, or at least all the trees and shrubs he had planted so lavishly. Anything shrubby or tree-like was put into those parts of the garden which were sheltered from the troublesome winds, mainly from the south-west. He gardened as he used to say 'above the knee', which was his way of saying that the little things which make a garden so lovely, such as primroses, bluebells, hardy cyclamens and daffodils, were merely extras in going from one delectable shrub to another. He would stride through lowly flowers with impunity, to point out to me yet another tender rarity. His greatest love was I think the whole family of magnolias. However he did not know or grow *Magnolia* x *thompsoniana*, deliciously scented and flowering in June. This was speedily put in one of the smaller walled gardens which he had not filled.

Previous owners had planted great shelter-belts but, owing to the exposure on the tip of Cornwall, many of the trees, beeches in particular, had grown into clumsy, forked specimens and it was obvious that the time was not far distant when many would fall. We all saw the necessity of planting new shelter-belts for the future, among them fast-growing maritime pines. Some of these were just in time to break the gales of the last century.

As a rule we started our tour down by the entrance gate reaching the house in time for lunch. As likely as not, Sir Edward would nod over his cup of coffee and I would steal out of the door and start absorbing the riches around the house – and there were many. One rarity which I never saw in any other garden was *Schima* subsp. *wallichii* var. *khasiana*, from north-east India. Fleshy yellow flowers hang from the drooping branches in autumn. In the sunny porch grew *Kennedia rubicunda*, and all around the sheltering house walls were *Dendromecon rigida*,

Tibouchina, Berberidopsis, callistemons and daturas. And in full sun across the lawn was *Rhododendron griersonianum,* which had to be clipped over after flowering to keep it compact.

Rhododendrons were I suppose Sir Edward's second great delight, and, like many other great gardeners, he could not resist making his own hybrids. Thus we have some very beautiful named crosses such as 'Laerdal', 'Morvah', 'Bulldog' and others.

The whole garden in spring is enlivened with scented rhododendrons, of the tender Maddenii Series. But Sir Edward did not only plant for spring. There are hundreds of blue hydrangeas, masses of nerines, *Schizostylis* in red and pink, hedychiums and more delights than I can cram into these pages. There is no doubt that he loved his garden and gloried in all sorts of plants – above the knee.

EDWARD AUGUSTUS BOWLES

Myddelton House
ENFIELD • MIDDLESEX
Lee Valley Regional Park Authority

E.A. BOWLES's name and expertise had long been known to me before I became involved in any capacity with the Royal Horticultural Society, which I joined I think about 1928. His name was always spoken with reverence due to his astonishing knowledge of all kinds of plants grown in our gardens. During his long life (he died at the age of eighty-nine in 1953) he was chairman of numerous committees of the RHS and honoured by many awards. He lived at Myddelton House, Enfield, and I remember that in most years our Superintendent at Cambridge spent part of his travelling allowance on a visit to his garden. This alone made me realize it was an important garden to visit. But it was not until I had a car in the late 1930s that I was able to do so. I found a lovely Georgian house (with no mod cons) which had belonged to his father, in the midst of a large garden with many trees and a vast collection of plants, guarded by Sir Hugh Myddelton's New River now nearly four hundred years old. Though it went through the garden and made a very interesting feature it produced no moisture for the plants, being so well made from the thickly puddled clay with which it was lined. There were however two ponds which enabled Bowles to grow water and bog plants; otherwise the garden was on gravel, but the shade cast by the big old trees prevented it from becoming too dry. He spent some sixty years amassing his loved plants, trees, shrubs, perennials, annuals and bulbs in beds and borders and in a rock garden and in fact practising horticulture exhaustively and with energy. He also had a conservatory and greenhouses.

After the Second World War I took three friends to see him; they were Iris (Lady) Lawrence, Gwendolyn Anley, both keen and knowledgeable gardeners, and Norman Gould, botanist at Wisley. We were told to bring baskets, with his usual generous intentions. I have written about this before (*Three Gardens*, 1983), how after going round the garden for a couple of hours we were invited in for tea. The ladies were shown upstairs for a wash and Norman and I went into the downstairs cloakroom. We entered the drawing room before the ladies and EAB asked us whether we had noticed the moss growing out of a crack in the lavatory pan. We said we had and he exclaimed, 'I'm *so* excited about it! It is a very rare British species!' The love of

Helleborus 'Bowles's Yellow'

plants could hardly go farther than that and it goes to show what a dedicated plantsman he was.

Whenever I visited him there were usually vases or pots with separate blooms in them in the hall. Only by seeing them daily in passing at close quarters could he get to know their beauty well and could transfer their loveliness by pencil or watercolours to paper. Thus he was able to illustrate his books (on crocuses, colchicums and daffodils) with his own works of art which I always rank with the most life-like portrayals of flowers ever achieved by anyone. And he gave as much care to the foliage – and sometimes even the root as well – as to the flowers.

So there we had over sixty years or more of gardening experience in every way presented to us with keen enjoyment and loving care. He extended his care to the boys in his neighbourhood by his Sunday school. Some remained friends for life.

He gave me many treasures over the years, particularly snowdrops; in fact he may be said to have been one of the first to collect, grow and illustrate many species and forms in such lifelike portraits that they have been reproduced several times, being treasured by the RHS in whose hands they reside.

E.A. Bowles was perhaps the greatest gardener mentioned in these pages and is outstanding for his prodigious knowledge, expertise and kindness. You have only to read again, not only the books he wrote which I have mentioned above, but his famous trilogy *My Garden in Spring, in Summer,* and *in Autumn and Winter* which are illustrated by black-and-white photographs of his garden and also by coloured pictures by various artists. In the first edition these include a number of photographs of flowers hand-coloured by T. Ernest Waltham which also graced the excellent handbooks on various genera in the *Present Day Gardening Series* published by *The Gardener's Chronicle* in the early years of the century. In many ways they struck a very high note in colour printing. The three books are written with a light but erudite touch and remind me so much of his conversation and anecdotes when walking round his garden.

These little paragraphs would not be complete without reference to *Rosa moschata*. In my researches into the genus in the early 1950s I discovered that the labels for this plant at Kew and Cambridge were placed in front of a different species, *R. brunonii*, a gigantic climber from the Himalaya which flowered only at midsummer, a confusion perpetrated by numerous botanists and authors. The Musk Rose on the other hand flowers from late summer onwards into autumn. I have only found this in two gardens: one was Myddelton, where it grew on the sunny wall of the house, and the other was Levens Hall in Cumbria. It has been recorded as a native of various countries in south Europe and Asia. Bowles had received his plant from Canon Ellacombe at Bitton Vicarage, Gloucestershire, and now this is the plant that is once more grown true to name; it has had an immense influence in rose breeding. (Recent research has proved that the Asiatic species, *R. fedtschenkoana* has had a similar influence through the ancient damask roses.) So we owe to Bowles the preservation of this historic rose through the century. And no doubt his generosity has echoes in numerous other plants and bulbs in various gardens in this and other countries. So the love of plants and flowers goes on, fostered by the keen spirits which gardening seems to breed.

MAJOR HENRY R. BROUGHTON, SECOND BARON FAIRHAVEN

Fairhaven Woodland and Water Garden
SOUTH WALSHAM • NORFOLK
Fairhaven Garden Trust

SELDOM DO TWO BROTHERS both have a leaning towards great gardening, but this is what happened to Huttleston and Henry Broughton who both inherited fortunes from their father who had emigrated to the United States. While Huttleston gave his fortune and energies to creating Anglesey Abbey in Cambridgeshire (see page 90), Major Henry R. Broughton gardened skilfully at Bakeham House, Englefield Green, Surrey. He used to come for plants to me as manager of a large nursery in the Woking area. One day he wanted dozens and dozens of various *Gentiana* species for a new bed he was preparing alongside a small stream. Fortunately we were able to supply.

Both he and his brother kept horses at Newmarket and so, on the tragic early death of his wife, Henry moved to South Walsham Hall, Norfolk. It is in the Broads area and he at once started making a garden there. I visited it one summer day when astilbes were in flower and realized that here there was going to be a great garden. Before he died in 1973 he had succeeded, with the help of several gardeners, in bringing the whole area, some 350 acres, under control. The Inner Broad acts as a starting point for the semi-wooded landscape planted with trees and shrubs and plants which he raised in his own nursery. He worked tirelessly to create beauty.

Today there are literally thousands of Asiatic primulas, mostly *P.P. bulleyana, pulverulenta* and *japonica* which produce a sight of rare enchantment. Bog arums, or *Lysichiton* (which people persist in calling skunk cabbage, which is really the vernacular name for *Symplocarpus foetidus*), poke their yellow noses out of the muddy margins of walks and streams.

But winter is really the start, while work is going on coppicing the hazels and clearing ditches in preparation for the February display of snowdrops, followed by early and late daffodils, primroses and bluebells, and so to the primulas and irises, and astilbes which appear in early and late summer, together with rhododendrons and scented azaleas, *Cornus* and *Philadelphus*, orchids and willow herb, extending later into many-tinted hydrangeas and giant lilies.

Although my paragraphs read like a description of any garden in the cooler, moister parts of the country, I should be wrong in leaving such an impression on the reader and visitor. It is not only a 'woodland and water garden' but the home to much wild life — birds, small animals, butterflies — including some rarities. Then there is the seasonal work going on in nursery and garden, together with the production of Christmas trees and wreaths, the coppicing of hazels for peasticks and the like. I am sure there is never a dull moment, which is what Lord Fairhaven would have wished.

I remember him as a dapper individual, with impeccably creased trousers and polished shoes, so that I can hardly imagine him in rough clothes for gardening, but he was an industrious worker and has left us with a piece of beautiful natural scenery, embellished richly and safeguarded for the future.

HUTTLESTON BROUGHTON, FIRST BARON FAIRHAVEN

Anglesey Abbey
CAMBRIDGESHIRE
National Trust

HUTTLESTON BROUGHTON WAS EDUCATED partly in the United States and partly at Harrow. He purchased Anglesey Abbey in 1926 and from then until his death in 1966 spent most of his time pursuing beauty in many different ways. Though he planted roses, perennials, spring bulbs and a number of distinctive trees and shrubs, he was not a typical English plantsman, but enjoyed the effect of trees and plants in the mass. As a consequence, on acquiring Anglesey, which is on flat land with no scenic beauty except distance and the changing light on the long days, he began his creation of the very large garden by planting many hundreds – in fact thousands – of native trees and bushes which he could see would grow well there. These fairly quickly gave him the protection from the winds which was essential, and enclosed the many large areas including what amounts to some thirty-five acres of mown grass. In this spacious setting he founded a large modern garden divided into small and large areas by hedges and spinneys. Each one has its own particular beauty focused on noble statuary, vases and urns.

These great ornaments in marble, stone or bronze were acquired over the years, turning the garden into a rich gathering of great works of art, each with a history of its own. With his sporting interests, his library, his belts of trees, his gardens of separate flowers, these great masterpieces give a unique aspect to the garden as a whole. Perhaps influenced by a line of Lombardy poplars leading to a neighbouring mill and planted on the bank of the river to commemorate Queen Victoria's Golden Jubilee of 1887, Lord Fairhaven had almost a passion for straight lines and avenues of trees. It was undoubtedly a good way of shaping the flat landscape. And so he planted another line of poplars, later adding an avenue of limes, a long walk confined by evergreen conifers and a short avenue of holm oaks. A long narrow avenue of elms was put in crossing the entire garden and underplanted with daffodils, but the elm disease defeated the intentions here and the elms have been replaced with hornbeams. And then, to commemorate the Coronation of George VI and Queen Elizabeth in 1937, an extensive avenue was planted with crossing avenues at the far end. The trees used here were London plane alternating with horse chestnut in four rows, copying that planted in Windsor Great Park. The intention was to reduce the avenue to one kind of tree, according to their progress. The chestnuts won, owing to a great storm in 1968 when the planes suffered severe damage and even uprooting.

It is a wonderfully relaxing garden to visit. To see all of it would take a whole morning, or even a whole day. The snowdrops and other early bulbs absorb one in February, followed by hosts of daffodils; and then, if you are fortunate in the date, April brings the scent of hyacinths, in blue and white: two thousand of them are planted annually, being followed later by short dahlias. The great D-shaped herbaceous garden is in beauty in June and July; the surrounding borders are twelve feet across punctuated by seats and clipped box bushes, with a long view to the mill down the straight side of the D. More dahlias in several colours are in a gently curved border. All this is of course followed by the autumn colour. But at every turn you find a special statue, bust, or – a great feature of the garden – the 'Temple' composed of ten majestic Corinthian columns brought from Chesterfield House in London. They guard, with their attendant yew hedges, a splendid statue of David about to launch his sling.

Soon after the National Trust had accepted Anglesey Abbey I was taken to see the garden and meet the head gardener. My colleague and I were given lunch and I remember having a glass of the most refreshing water I had ever tasted. On another occasion I asked for it again but was saddened by being refused it: 'We are now on the mains, Sir.' Natural water or mains, they were great days, going round with the head gardener, Noel Ayres, and gradually getting to know the many acres and their plantings.

We tried to keep the garden as Huttleston left it. We did plant a few less usual trees in an extensive, almost empty square lawn. Ayres evinced no enthusiasm, so I said, in a facetious way, 'It will make mowing easier.' He merely answered, 'Yes,' in a mournful tone.

SIR JAMES AND LADY BURNETT OF LEYS

Crathes Castle
KINCARDINESHIRE • SCOTLAND
National Trust for Scotland

CRATHES CASTLE and its famous garden had haunted me for many years before I managed to find the time to travel so far north to see it. It has a magical approach through woodland and great trees, especially beech and lindens which were in the full beauty of their young summer foliage. Lady Burnett had given me a special invitation to visit their much loved home and was waiting with Sir James on that sparkling morning to take me round the garden.

The castle was an impressive first sight of all the glory and history that has built up in it since its foundation in the sixteenth century. Its treasures go back to a hunting horn presented by Robert the Bruce in the fourteenth century to one in the long line of Burnetts.

Just below the castle are some very old yew hedges, now perhaps too fat and spreading. Otherwise the garden is a series of formal walled enclosures in which different schemes were developed by Lady Burnett during the twentieth century. While Sir James was deeply interested in trees and shrubs, Lady Burnett specialized in devising colour effects from a unique range of herbaceous plants, including those noted for their foliage, and it is these with which these short notes are mainly concerned.

I knew Gertrude Jekyll and had seen several of her colour borders and I was interested that she had been to Crathes and approved of the plantings there. Her graded colour schemes may have inspired Lady Burnett in the first place. They inspired many garden plantings of the period including Hidcote, Mount Stewart and Tintinhull, but Sybil Burnett had her own ideas about working with colours in the garden. I was completely bowled over by the originality and gorgeous effect in a small formal garden below the castle. She had cleverly used the soft pinky-brown stone walls to add a background to which all flower colours contributed their bit. Flaming reds with large black eyes were given by *Papaver commutatum* and one would have thought that this would have been the dominant key-colour; but no, it was only a contributing factor in the general scheme which included other reds and even magenta-tinted pinks and reds (I remember *Rosa gallica* var. *officinalis*), some yellows and intermediate tints, from tall plants down to creeping thymes, which were given slabs of rosy-brown stone to creep over. All colours were given companions of what we call coppery leaves – *Cotinus, Berberis* and others. This was the first master stroke; it unified the whole scheme and linked it to the colour of the stone walls. (We should rightly call this coppery foliage murrey-coloured, the colour of mulberry juice; it is not described by 'copper' or 'purple'.) This garden, in addition to its surrounding borders, also had a main planting of colour centred around a square still pool guarded by four L-shaped dark yew hedges, so that the smoothness of the water was appreciated only from certain angles. There was a great prolificity of colours and shapes wherever you looked and so I think it will be realized what an unblemished conception this was. It alone made the day and long journey well worthwhile. I have never seen another garden with even half the magic of this. (My photograph of it is reproduced in my *The Art of Planting*, 1984.)

But there were other thrills as well. With its four paths meeting under an ancient mushroom-shaped Portugal laurel there is the White Garden. I fancy this must be the oldest White Garden in these islands, pre-dating Sissinghurst, Barrington Court and the little effort at Hidcote. Apart from white and nearly white flowers there is silver foliage and the other supreme touch at Crathes: the four longer borders are backed by murrey-coloured hedges of *Prunus cerasifera* 'Pissardii'. Need I say more?

There are other fascinating borders devoted to certain colours, or should I say that each is made distinct by having one colour excluded? Two borders are superb in early summer leading down to the little dovecote; they start at a small hedged corner where grows a form of *Hosta tokudama* whose grey blue leaves are irregularly striped with green. I had never seen it before but came across it later in Lady Moore's garden at Rathfarnham, Dublin.

As if this is not enough – and all the time we are passing very choice shrubs of Sir James's gathering, such as *Philadelphus delavayi*, *Eleutherococcus trifoliatus*, *Clematoclethra integrifolia* and *Davidia* – there are beds below it all devoted to a later summer display of blue flowers, mostly annuals but enriched by *Salvia patens*.

Being one of the most individual gardens in these islands – and not just a planted woodland – it is splendid to see it so well kept by the Trust. With its picturesque rosy-brown turrets, the castle looks down upon it all. Untold joys are inside as well and we bless the Burnetts for all they did for us. Most of the planting had been done since 1950, at a time when staff became scarce and we all thought nothing would be the same again. The Burnetts proved us wrong.

WARWICK AND PHYLLIS DEEPING

Eastlands
WEYBRIDGE • SURREY
National Trust

IT MAY SURPRISE some readers to see this famous novelist of the early part of the century included in these pages. His most famous book *Sorrell and Sons* appeared in 1925 and was immediately a great success, in fact a bestseller, and, among other titles, enabled him to purchase an old house at Weybridge, Surrey, and to add to the area of garden from time to time. He wanted seclusion and secured it because the house was far from the road with trees all round it. But this was not all; he erected closely woven panels of trellis to some ten feet above the front fence. He was amused to hear the locals discussing it outside the garden: 'They say he is going to advertise his books on it!' The longish drive led up to the front of the house and then on to a separate garage and a large area for vegetables. He also had a cool greenhouse where he grew luscious plums, nectarines and cherries in pots so that the fruits could be picked at the acme of perfection for dessert. No bought fruits could compare. When the Second World War started, he purchased (or rented) a small local farm where he produced wheat, potatoes, onions and so forth.

One day in the mid-1930s he arrived at the wholesale nursery where I was manager and, after the customary civilities were over, announced that he wanted 'a hundred rhododendrons'.

Being a wholesale nurseryman I was used to such requests but the fact that it was a retail order astonished me. We inspected the rhododendron field (they were not in flower as it was autumn) and my order book was soon filled. He came several more times for other plants and on one occasion brought his wife, Phyllis. While Warwick was more interested in the big things and fruit and vegetables, she was always on the lookout for beauty. She had an artist's eye for colour and form. I still have a picture of hers, a beautiful trio of roses embroidered in wool. And not just of wool off the skein or ball, but pulled to pieces and used as single threads, dyed if necessary to achieve the right tint. She carried her thoughts into the garden. She did not go in for Jekyllian colour schemes but planted her beds and borders annually for summer display – after the spring upsurge of beauty – with careful mixtures of bright colours which held the eyes from too many tall and dusky pines. I remember also a border devoted to a gorgeous mixture of phloxes.

We became close friends and I attended lovely tennis parties (he had a very good serve) on their hard court, with strawberries or raspberries – from the garden – and cream for tea.

But he was the designer of the garden and had the wit and ability to build a small temple out of concrete at the end of one of the walks. The pillars were fluted, the mixture being set to dry in rolls of narrowly corrugated iron. I wonder if this has been repeated by anyone? There were balustrades and steps and paved areas all well arranged and suited to the gently sloping ground.

Phyllis lived for some years after Warwick's death and she erected a plaque to his memory on the house, Eastlands, which she left to the National Trust. She was a good pianist but achieved the effect in a way that I had never before come across: the loud pedal was kept down the whole time but the pressure on the notes was much varied. She played, correctly, the tune with the right hand from memory but had the skill to invent the bass as she went along. Her touch entranced all who heard it. I do not think she read music readily so we never played two-piano duets.

There was a magnificent full-length portrait of her in the dining room, painted in oils I think. She was depicted in emerald green to contrast with her auburn hair. I never saw her dressed in any other colour, summer or winter. Even her purse, notebook, pencil and shoelaces were dyed to match. I have often wondered whether Warwick ever tired of it.

It speaks well for Warwick's enthusiasm for horticulture that in his later years he wrote *Shabby Summer*. This was about a nurseryman who spent his life growing plants with the usual vicissitudes, especially the weather. I was told at the time by a mutual friend that I had inspired the story!

RALPH DUTTON, LORD SHERBORNE

Hinton Ampner
ALRESFORD • HAMPSHIRE
National Trust

MANY YEARS AGO I knew an ardent gardener who was always keen to hear of the newest and brightest plants, all verging towards reds and scarlets. She pursued these colours with avidity. After some years she took a friend to live with her who was a very keen flower arranger delighting in cool and subtle colours. Over a few years my gardening friend gave up searching for and planting strong colours, having had her eyes opened by her companion. Henceforth her garden plants were changed, no doubt giving her less excitement but more tranquillity. This was just what Ralph Dutton also desired, above all else, in a garden, and I think there is no doubt that he achieved it.

He had studied the art of gardening deeply as is proved by the book he wrote on *The English Garden* (1937) when he was thirty-nine years old. It remains not only one of the first books on the history of garden art but a seminal work unsurpassed by the many that have followed, and it is a well-illustrated handbook – not of the coffee table variety. But he was an expert also in all the pursuits that go to make a home-lover: not only architecture and connoisseurship of all that is beautiful indoors, but also the design and decoration of a garden, and moreover he had a wonderful insight into park planting, generally a lost art today. He left his house and contents, his garden and 1,650 acres of the estate to the National Trust in 1985. While the National Trust has of course been given larger houses and estates I always feel that Hinton Ampner in Hampshire is unique among such bequests in being almost entirely the product of one brain.

Ralph inherited Hinton in 1935 and immediately decided to turn the elaborate, gabled Victorian mansion into one which had sober Georgian features; he also developed the garden. He was, however, to suffer a major disaster. The house caught fire on a windy, dry, spring day in 1960 and was speedily gutted; he lost many precious possessions. Undeterred he at once decided to rebuild and refurnish and in three years he was able to say that his home was 'once again fully habitable'. He was a man of great knowledge in all walks of life, and of a determined and capable mind, modest and retiring.

I had heard for some years of the charm of his garden. While beautifully situated in delightful, rolling countryside it is on a hungry chalk soil where only certain plants grow well. The approach drive even goes through clumps of trees planted by Ralph. The south front, directly you step out of the house, shows the benefit of the site, sheltered from the north by trees and rising ground, and tender shrubs such as *Pittosporum* and *Hebe* thrive. But no amount of choice plants can rival the invitation to stroll up the wide grass walk to the statue and broad view beyond.

There is something imperturbable and restful about a grass walk measured by the placing of dark green sentries of Irish yews along both sides. They are perhaps now getting rather stout, but not so that you cannot see well between them how the soft-coloured flowers complement the feeling. I have long wondered what prompted a further length of yews, English this time, clipped carefully into cones supporting tops which make them look something like staddle stones. But no, the shape, unique I believe in British gardens, is something which has developed from slim cones with knobs at their tops. One of the walks is less formal and is planted lavishly with old French roses. These were what brought us together in the first place.

The ground had been formalized and terraced in a variety of ways and all is carefully planted in quiet colours with superb views out into the park but also intriguingly inwards to the next feature. There is a charming classical temple, set amongst a background of shrubs and focused on an ancient short avenue of leaning lime trees guarding a stone obelisk. Turning various corners and up certain steps the visitor will have two more surprises. There is a deep dell filled with handsome foliage plants, with mighty shrubs and trees overwhelmed in July by cascades of *Synstylae* roses, including *R. filipes* 'Kiftsgate', a single white species of delicious fragrance. A still greater surprise is found where the soil is not limy, and there grow rhododendrons and allied plants.

I have been to Hinton on many occasions and have never been disappointed. The garden joys are kept up well through the seasons. It is tranquil and Ralph's courteous and unassuming hospitality remains a truly happy memory. He helped us with the gardens of the National Trust with an all-seeing eye and capable brain.

LEONARD AND DOROTHY ELMHIRST

Dartington Hall
TOTNES • DEVON
Dartington Hall Trust

THESE TWO WORTHY FOLK were each deeply interested in architecture, trees and the countryside, with strong leanings towards art in general. It so happens that they paid a visit to the wholesale nursery where I was working about 1935, ten years after they had purchased Dartington Hall, and I detected Dorothy's deep interest in plants and gardening matters. Little did I think that over sixty years later I should be writing about Dorothy's garden, and realizing what a wonderful job they did in everything concerned with the old foundation – one of the very oldest to remain more or less intact until today. Dorothy had almost unlimited means (she was an American) and they both deeply appreciated the rolling Devon terrain, the ancient building and the old trees. Between them over many years they gradually brought the Hall to new life and beauty, and gave it a deep reason. They worked hard to create beauty everywhere and the name of Dartington became synonymous with high ideals and many of the great arts. During one of their courses I was honoured by being asked to lecture to the assembly, probably about roses or the gardens of the National Trust. It was an evening of great pleasure.

To be confronted by a run-down garden and building was rather more than they could cope with in young middle age, so they consulted H. Avray Tipping, who had done so much in an advisory capacity and through his writings about historic gardens and houses in *Country Life*. He sketched out the main bones of the garden and then gracefully excused himself of more. Dorothy, feeling still in need of guidance – or at least discussion – asked the famous American horticulturist Beatrix Farrand to come over to England and give the benefit of her advice. Much was accomplished under her guidance over several years, until she became too old to travel. After that, they secured the services of Percy Cane, a well-known garden designer. I have seen several of Percy Cane's gardens; some features are rather repetitive, but 'spacious' applies to all, I think. He was the right professional expert to employ. The result today shows something of all their work, but it is unified in the spaciousness that the Elmhirsts desired. There is no doubt that over the many acres this was the overriding aim. Through all the years Dorothy was the *arbiter elegantiae*.

The many old trees – some, the sweet chestnuts, still standing – have been nurtured or pruned or replaced and since it is now run by a Trust should be good for many years to come. There is no doubt that the Elmhirsts did wonderful work and their industry in every way secured a unique holding for us all.

Everything is spacious at Dartington. It is a large building with a widespread courtyard and imposing entrance and is a genuine old fabric, lived in by one family, the Champernownes, for almost four hundred years but built before then for the half-brother of Richard II, near the Saxon burgh of Totnes. The great group of buildings, the tilt yard and the noble row of Irish yews were the foundations on which the Elmhirsts fostered their imaginations – he with his deep interest in forestry and agriculture and she with her sense of beauty through gardening. How fortunate we are that their high ideals are protected by a Trust. Dartington has become synonymous with the arts and all things worthy of deep attention. Long may it survive and attract serious-minded people.

BETTY FARQUHAR

Ardsallagh
TIPPERARY • EIRE
Privately owned

ON A GLORIOUS EARLY SUMMER DAY Helen Dillon motored Rosemary Brown, David Shackleton and myself to Ardsallagh, the home and garden of Betty Farquhar. The long journey had ample rewards. The drive took us to an imposing grey stone house and we were welcomed by Betty and taken through her beautiful drawing room into the sun-drenched garden which she had laid out over the years. She was fortunate to have plenty of stone locally to aid her in making a series of formal gardens, in a setting of thick old walls and arched doorways.

Apart from a wide selection of shrubs and climbers on the house walls, we were well rewarded with the views across and around a large formal garden surrounded with low walls holding up the soil for a collection of beautiful alpines, dwarf shrubs and other plants. The way then took us to another walled enclosure with a central formal pool in which were many water-lilies and again retaining walls holding up the surrounding beds, lavishly filled with all manner of choice plants and shrubs.

Yet another door, it seems to me, took us to a wide paved path with low foot-high walls holding up two magnificent herbaceous borders. I had not seen anything like them before; low-growing and creeping plants spread over the little walls while the major planting of the raised borders brought the massed flowers to eye-level and of course above it to some six feet. The riot of colour and form took a lot of study and revealed early yuccas in flower and several South African annuals. We rather felt we had seen the garden by this time, but no, away behind the glory was a grouping of rare and lovely shrubs to flower throughout the year.

We then entered a spacious courtyard next to the house and sat ourselves down in easy chairs round a small table in the dappled shade cast by a large *Eucalyptus globulus*. We were able to look around while tea was being brought and found that every windowsill and ledge was supporting pots of colourful geraniums, fuchsias and the like, with here and there a rare climbing plant ascending the walls. *Dregea sinensis* (syn. *Wattakaka sinensis*) was a-drip with its clusters of white stars. *Jasminum polyanthum*, a winter-flowering tender species, was producing a few late flowers and scenting the air, and several tall forms of ivy-leaved pelargoniums ascended the walls with mutisias and the shining leaves of *Clematis armandii*. The whole of this sheltered, flowery court made us think we were in the much warmer climate of southern Spain or Italy. It was a most wonderful and refreshing spell after the hot walk round the garden areas.

It had been something of a surprise to find such a rich assembly of plants arranged so that they benefited from the several different exposures in sun or shade; each plant grown well for its individual merit and beauty. There were no Jekyllian colour schemes. But when we eventually got up to take our leave, I could not resist the temptation and desire to see the drawing room again, for there was Betty's colour sense revealed. I have never seen a room in which soft colours were grouped to such advantage. There was no lack of colour; it was a highly satisfying room. But all colours were muted and tinted down to an overall softness that left me spellbound.

REGINALD FARRER

INGLEBOROUGH • YORKSHIRE
Privately owned

BEFORE I HAD TAKEN to gardening professionally I had 'fallen under the spell of Farrer's wonderful pen' – as someone at the time put it. It so happened there were two lending libraries in Cambridge; one had *The English Rock Garden* (1919) and the other *The Dolomites* (1913) both by Farrer. The former was published in the Present Day Gardening Series and was a small how-to-do-it volume; like all in the series it was well illustrated in colour from watercolours on black-and-white photographs by T. Ernest Waltham. They were vivid and compelling. The second book was much larger and deeply interesting likewise, with coloured photographs of some plants, but mainly of startling rocky eminences and mountains. I borrowed them again and again. Kind friends with cars took me to famous nurseries specializing in alpine plants – Clarence Elliott's Six

Hills Nursery at Stevenage and Gavin Jones's at Letchworth; and of course, right on my doorstep, Casburn and Welch at Cambridge. This was all very fortunate for one whose main aim, at the time, was alpine plants and rock gardens.

Farrer went on to write a series of excellent books on alpine plants, including three on his travels in eastern Asia until his early and sad death far away from everything but rain in Upper Burma, as recorded in *Farrer's Last Journey* by E.H.M. Cox.

He gardened in a wet part of the country in the district near Ingleborough, north-western Yorkshire. Not only did he have a garden but he went to much trouble to acclimatize European alpines on the rocky face of Ingleborough. He brought quantities of lovely pieces of rock from the hills to beautify his own garden, but did not grasp the significance of the stratification and placing of rocks in a natural manner. But his enthusiasm for and absorption of the plants from high places came second to none.

He was friendly with the other great rock plant enthusiasts and cultivators, Henri Correvon of Geneva and F. Sündermann at Lindau Bodensee in Bavaria. What a lot has grown out of their skill and enthusiasm! It is as well to recall here that earlier gardeners and botanists did not take readily to going in search of garden plants on the mountains; the meadows and lower alps enthralled them sufficiently. Thus the correct placing of rocks was not understood until Captain B.H.B. Symons-Jeune put up some exhibits at Chelsea Show in 1923 and subsequently. His book *Natural Rock Gardening* appeared in 1932.

For some obscure reason the professional rock garden makers took no real notice and nothing further appeared in books until my *The Rock Garden and its Plants* (1989).

But this is scarcely applicable to what are really only a few paragraphs about Reginald Farrer. I have written the above because Farrer was in the forefront of what was the new

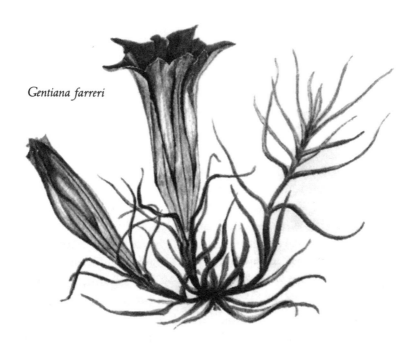

Gentiana farreri

enthusiasm for alpines. He was enthralled by them – from very dwarf shrubs and bog plants to his marvellous penmanship about the 'Children of the Hills'. There is no doubt that without Farrer to guide and infect us the cult of the alpine plant would not have got so far so fast. I have never forgotten my first reading of his description of one of his most significant discoveries in eastern Asia. Here it is remembered, engraved on my memory for three-quarters of a century: *Gentiana farreri* 'of a fierce and luminous Cambridge blue within, while without, long vandykes of periwinkle purple alternate with swelling panels of nankeen, with a violet median line'. It is true and gives us all something to think about. My portrait of the authentic species was painted in 1928. We could do with a few more Reginald Farrers.

MARK FENWICK

Abbotswood
STOW-ON-THE-WOLD • GLOUCESTERSHIRE
Dikler Farming Company

BY ABOUT 1927 I felt it was time that I should see other parts
of England besides the Norfolk coast in the holidays. I think
my mother felt the same for she readily assented when the
proposition was put to her of a visit to the Cotswolds. Who is
there that is not captivated by the architecture and hills of that
region? As a contrast to the slate roofs at home, with very
gentle incline, the steep gables of the stone belt – occasioned
by the weight of the thick stone tiles – came as a sort of
glorious relief and change, while the colour of the stone, so
different from the white or occasionally red bricks of
Cambridge, was also a novel change. The architecture alone,
ready for pencil sketching, was a longed-for treat. But there was
another special urge: I had been introduced at a Royal
Horticultural Society show to Fred Tustin, the head gardener at
Mr Mark Fenwick's famous garden, who had invited me to go
to the garden if anywhere near.

And so we went and stayed at the pleasant little town of
Stow-on-the-Wold and Abbotswood was only just down the
hill. It was early September but there was still much to see, and
apart from a Lutyens garden near Cromer I had seen nothing
of the country's great gardens. Abbotswood was a mental uplift
and doubly interesting by being introduced to it by Mr Tustin.

What a revelation it was! Everything was in apple-pie order. The drive leading down to the splendid gabled house, with shrubs and plants on every side; the cunning stone sconce under one of the gables pouring forth a little stream of water into the pool – with reflections from the water on to the masonry – and the water-lilies; the magnificent arrangement on the lawn of beds bright with all sorts of short perennials; the rose garden disporting hard-pruned bushes in flower of the then new Hybrid Musk roses; the water garden leading away downhill with trees and shrubs everywhere; and the biggest surprise of all, a large area covered with all sorts of heaths and heathers! And this was on limy soil. Mr Tustin explained to me that the winter-flowering heaths would tolerate a certain amount of lime if fed with plenty of humus. But it was the great glory of the large and lovely garden that literally enthralled me.

I had the great pleasure of meeting Mr Fenwick too. He was not only a knowledgeable plantsman (he served on some RHS committees) but also knew all about gardening and exhibiting. He had been laying out the garden and altering the house with the aid of Edwin Lutyens and between them they brought a superlative garden into being. It only just scrapes into this book having been started before 1900.

On subsequent visits Mr Tustin would take me round a bend among shrubs, and there would be a shrub at its perfect best. Tustin would be silent for a moment and then, 'Ah, that's a very fine piece,' he would say with the greatest satisfaction. I have seen him tying with finest strips of bass each bud on a clematis so that all the flowers would be equidistant. He had time to be perfect. And for tea there would be 'Royal Sovereign' strawberries accompanied by rows of the thinnest crustless bread and butter. There was never a disappointment in anything at Abbotswood.

The years rolled by and in due course Mr and Mrs Harry Ferguson acquired the property. His tractors were displayed on the lawns. Mrs Ferguson was very keen and thrilled with the beauty of the garden and did not at first want to alter it. But the time came when she decided on certain adjustments. In the gaps between the pillars of the pergolas on one side, next to the rose garden, were five Ali Baba olive-oil jars which she did not like. It so happened that my friend Jim Russell heard of this and purchased them for a garden he was designing, but he only wanted four. Would I like the odd one? I was just making my first garden near Woking and accepted without hesitation. It is in my garden to this day, reminding me of many happy visits.

On one of my later visits Ruby Fleischmann (see page 112) was also present and we all four (with Tustin) went round the garden together. Mrs Ferguson made some remark about the garden not being quite so tidy as usual because 'my gardener has not been well'. I turned to Tustin and expressed sorrow and hoped he would soon be quite well again. With a slightly acid look he said meaningfully, 'Our *gardener.*' This was the first intimation I had had that he, Tustin, had more or less retired. We still kept in touch with Christmas cards after he had fully retired and had gone to live with his daughter.

The selection of *Nerine bowdenii* known as 'Mark Fenwick' is still the best hardy form to grow against your sunny walls, but preferably not red brick, which wars with the clear pink autumn flowers.

Mine came direct from Fred Tustin. He was a grand old man and great expert; one of the old school.

RUBY FLEISCHMANN

Chetwode Manor
BUCKINGHAM
Privately owned

RUBY'S HUSBAND was on the stock exchange with Colonel
Messel of Nymans (see page 174) and I fancy that Ruby's
enthusiasm for old French roses was engendered by Maud
Messel. On hearing of my growing appreciation of the old
roses Bobby Jenkinson of Knap Hill said I should go to
Chetwode Manor, near Buckingham, to see Ruby's collection.
It was just after the war, one lovely Saturday afternoon. The
Manor was a fair-sized farm, on very heavy clay soil and open
to almost all the winds that blow. But here Ruby had produced
a good garden protected from the east and north by a huge
beech hedge. She was deeply steeped in the history of garden
design and had made a large parterre of beds and surrounding
straight borders, all filled with delectable plants.

A great weeping willow was a quick-growing screen to
shut out the modern wing of the old manor house. The
parterre was marked out by strategically placed cones of
golden privet supported by dwarf box hedges. I think the
privet was chosen to brighten the winter effect because the
windows of the house looked directly upon it. Each sectional
bed was filled with lovely flowers: campanulas, Belladonna
delphiniums, masses of seed-raised pinks in many colours,
stachys punctuated by old roses. Among many others it was

my first sight of the Damask 'Celsiana' and the only garden in England where I came across it; it was given to Ruby under the name of 'Cellini' but there was no mistaking its exact likeness to Redouté's portrait. There was another intriguing rose – which Ruby called 'Fantin-Latour'. I accepted the name at the time but subsequently found there was no rose named after the famous painter. It was so like the roses shown by him that I always think Ruby named it herself. It is now widely grown.

Besides the great parterre there was a shady cool border backed by pleached limes overspread and decorated by rambling and climbing roses of light colours. Some had ascended tall trees at the back. As if this was not enough there was a pair of borders of more roses of purplish and murrey colourings with white foxgloves and light blue delphiniums.

I met the two daughters, who were much taken by the beauty of flowers. After her husband died, Ruby moved to a smaller house at Batsford in the Cotswolds, and created another beautiful garden, but with fewer roses as the area was comparatively small. But she gathered a host of lovely plants for it and it was always, seemingly, in full flower at whatever time of the year I went. I particularly remember the variegated horseradish – a striking plant – and the genuine *Aster x frikartii* 'Mönch'. Owing to an injury to her back she could not do much actual gardening but defeated her infirmity by an ingenious device. It was a stablecomb fitted to the bottom of a walking stick which enabled her to go weeding! There was a long border devoted to all the yellow and orange flowers of summer; otherwise the colours were cool pinks, mauves and the colours of phloxes. A great new treasure was the hybrid lilac *Syringa x josiflexa* 'Bellicent'.

This little story would not be complete without reference again to Chetwode Manor. It was bought by a turkey farmer who kept his birds on the ground floor of the house. They pecked every plant and weed from the garden for several years. Eventually it was bought by Jennifer who married (later) Tim Collins and between them they have made a very lovely garden. After purchasing the manor and farm they were discussing between friends whom they could get to help them. My name was suggested, funnily enough, and I have once again helped with the same garden.

DR WILFRID FOX

Winkworth Arboretum
GODALMING • SURREY
National Trust

IN MY BOOK *Gardens of the National Trust*, I wrote the following: 'It is, I think, a wonderful thing, a magnanimous gesture, for someone to develop and plant such an area during the evening of his life, with the sole object of creating beauty and then to hand it to the Trust for the benefit of us all.'

Living as he did in a lovely old house in a valley near Godalming, Dr Fox must, I feel, have been entranced by the small landscape and lakes in the valley. From a vantage point above his house the morning light adds its glamour to the scene, which is lost after midday. Judging by the garden around his house, his kindness and hospitality (were there ever more tasty muscat grapes than off his sunny walls?), he must have long been interested in growing plants of all kinds, but it was obvious that as with so many gardeners who pass middle age successfully, trees and shrubs were his special delight.

The land he selected for his arboretum was poor, sandy and unfit for farming; the siting delightful, looking down on two lakes away to rising ground – outside his jurisdiction – chequered with small fields. In the sixty-five acres which he originally purchased he planted some belts of pines and larches to act as income for the future. The rest of the ground he planted with a wide variety of trees and shrubs mainly to give colour in autumn, but areas were set aside for azaleas in spring, shrubs for summer, and, for winter, a glade for conspicuous leaves. The bluebell wood studded with oaks he left alone except for a few Japanese maples. There was an old planting of cob nuts; these he left temporarily to act as nurses for young magnolias.

Work in the arboretum has gone on since he left us, including development and replanting. A certain amount of thinning and pruning was required and a memorial plaque was designed in his memory by Sir Hugh Casson, guarded by a pair of *Eucryphia* x *nymansensis* 'Nymansay'.

FRANK GALSWORTHY

CHERTSEY • SURREY

Soon after my arrival in Surrey a friend lent me John Galsworthy's famous *The Forsyte Saga* and its two sequels. It is a writing that has always enthralled me and I must have read the three volumes three or four times since. It was not until recent years that I noticed that the third volume, *The End of the Chapter*, was dedicated to Frank Galsworthy who, I believe, was his cousin. I have heard it said more than once that the family always pronounced the first syllable 'Gal' with a short 'a' to rhyme with shall. I was also told that when the two cousins met in the United States John announced that he had changed his name to rhyme with awl, because, he said, the long 'a' better suits the American intonation.

I had often heard about Frank who lived at nearby Chertsey and was a great watercolourist and lover of plants. I wanted to meet him and Gwendolyn Anley arranged this for me; I went over one Saturday afternoon and was welcomed and taken round a most intriguing garden full of all manner of plants. He lived alone but was well looked after by Jack Allam and his wife. While she ran the house and did the cooking, Jack became personal attendant, butler, chauffeur and head gardener of two. I visited on several occasions and in different seasons and saw wonderful collections of modern daffodils, auriculas and a huge range of primulas including several different forms of *Primula sieboldii*. There were irises of every shade, modern and old roses, through the gamut of garden plants of the whole year including many shrubs, all arranged in careful array in different corners. In spite of this the garden was very attractive. The larger collections of flowers were because Frank liked to record the whole variation of each genus and with primulas in particular – which were not grown easily in dry Surrey – he went to great trouble to paint in the natural background of their native habitats. The Royal Botanic Garden, Edinburgh, was most helpful in this respect.

The cultivation was under the watchful eye of Jack Allam and well he managed it all; he had his own little collection of sempervivums in pots. One day I had the luxury of going over when we had E.A. Bowles with us. 'Bowley' he called him, and 'Bowley knows everything' was one of his sayings.

They were both expert artists when it came to flowers. I always think that Bowles got as near to the perfection of an original flower as anyone had ever done, flower, foliage and often root as well. They both had a wonderful knack of making the shape of a curved petal with one stroke of the brush. Frank used a very wet brush and I have a painting of his of *Paeonia delavayi* which clearly shows not only the shape and colouring but the glossiness as well. He loved his flowers but got a bit bored with the foliage! Not so Bowles, who was of a botanical turn of mind as well as a great gardener at Enfield in Middlesex (see page 83).

Frank's house was, I think, two old cottages joined into one. He added a long corridor or hall at the back to unite them, and for hanging pictures and exhibiting his many treasures. If the weather was the least cold he wore a broad-brimmed hat and a cloak and carried a walking stick.

At one time he was very busy recording all the lilies he could acquire. *Lilium* x *testaceum* was a special joy to me, depicted with great verve, showing exactly the bold curve of the petals. He did something like three dozen lily species, and this was of course long before the hybrid races appeared; all the species came from Wallace of Tunbridge Wells and were made to grow in the garden.

The garden deteriorated in later years. Jack Allam was unable to do as much as previously and one gardener left. Even so, in his ninety-second year Frank decided to paint ninety-two fruits, berries and seedheads and to exhibit them at one of the Royal Horticultural Society shows. This he managed well; I took him a few fruits for inclusion. His greeting to me after the show was, 'Well, I've done it; it nearly killed me with the journeys and standing about, but I got my customary gold medal!'

Hearing that windmills were likely to disappear from our landscapes, he set about painting all he could find in the south of the country. These and many others of his paintings are preserved in the Chertsey Museum.

JOHN S.L. GILMOUR

Cambridge University Botanic Garden
CAMBRIDGE

JOHN WAS ONE OF THE LITTLE BAND of deeply enthused botanists who gained much of their inspiration from Humphrey Gilbert-Carter, the renowned and widely read Director of the Cambridge University Botanic Garden. He was director in my time at the garden and spoke several languages of different derivations.

I remember John at lectures and much later in the garden. On becoming a graduate he was given the post of Curator of the University Herbarium. His next move was to Kew where he became assistant director. Before I acquired a car it was an arduous journey, by bus from Chobham, train to Surbiton and bus again to Kew, where there was always a welcome for me from him and his parents. He wanted to get more enthusiastic about garden plants and asked me to help him build and stock a small rock garden in his garden. This was at Descanso House by the main road at Kew Gardens. While he was there he became engaged to and married Molly, a delightful girl who, he said, could play anything from Bach to jazz on the piano. Considering that music was, as for me, his second enthusiasm or hobby, it was a very lovely happening.

But the war followed and he was seconded to the Coal Board for its duration. The next move was to Wisley as director. This was only a few miles from Chobham and meant that we could meet frequently not only for the love of plants but for madrigal singing which was his and my great enthusiasm. We did it in the old style, around a large oval table with candles, wine and refreshments. He also reorganized many of the procedures at Wisley.

On the retirement of Humphrey Gilbert-Carter at Cambridge he became director, a post which I am sure he had wanted from early days. The appointment coincided with the realization of the munificent Cory Bequest. Reginald Cory was an old friend of the garden. He married the secretary and eventually left a vast sum to the under-endowed establishment. (When I was working there in the late 1920s, we had to put up with broken-down wheelbarrows and second-rate tools.) Cory had already given funds for the building of Cory Lodge in the middle of the garden, where the director lived. Fortunately there were several acres of land which were given to allotments for hire. An uncle of mine had one. The Cory Bequest meant that the allotments came to an end, the area was added to the garden, the greenhouses were repaired or rebuilt, a laboratory and lecture room were added and a very large rock garden was built around the pond. Much of it was built with great rocks of Westmorland limestone and cleverly divided into islands in the lawn, each island containing plants from a different part of the world, but there was also a goodly bank of Sussex sandstone built on imported lime-free soil. It is a wonderful effort made by the Superintendent, Robert W. Younger, but I always felt it was an unfortunate intrusion in the garden of 1836, which was of splendid design. (As I remember it, each corner of the great pathways was governed by a collection of evergreens – box or yews, conifers, hollies and so on.)

One of John's innovations was a garden of scented flowers and foliage laid out specially for the delectation of blind visitors; another a garden devoted to colour in winter; another an intriguing almost serpentine bed, with the planting clearly indicated by lengths devoted to plant introductions of each one hundred years of gardening history. A great fountain dominates the main lawn.

I lost touch with John and Molly after his retirement, but welcomed the new director, Dr Max Walters – another pupil of Gilbert-Carter's – and have continued visiting the garden whenever opportunity occurred. A special occasion was the celebration of its centenary when visitors assembled from all over the world, culminating in a dinner in King's College hall, where the King's Singers performed between courses. Max had asked me to join the party and to act as escort to the visits made by the concourse to famous gardens in East Anglia. We had five wonderful days together.

THE EARL AND COUNTESS OF HADDINGTON

Tyninghame
EAST LOTHIAN • SCOTLAND
Privately owned

HAVING BEEN INVITED to give a lecture some twenty-five years ago during the Charleston summer season by Lady Birley, I arrived as arranged on what was a particularly hot day — probably the hottest for some years. Lectures were given in an immense barn where there was little ventilation except by the door. It was very dark and the slides I used, photographs of gardens of the National Trust, showed up wonderfully on the large screen. I had an Anglepoise lamp focused on my notes which created intense heat around me. Never had I been so hot, but it was worth it for we were all given tea later in the lovely garden and there I met Lady Haddington. She gave me a pressing invitation to go to her garden the next time I was in Scotland. I took advantage of this kind invitation the following year and arrived on a clear and lovely summer's day. There had been heavy rain a week previously which had cleared the air and put new life into the plants. After lunch with her and the Earl, we went into the garden and I could not have seen it in better condition.

Tyninghame is a great, dominating and yet graceful Victorian building in soft rosy sandstone and it was quite obvious that Lady Haddington had a sure eye for use of colours. The large rose garden was planted with light yellow and white roses and other flowers with lots of silvery foliage plants. On the other side of the mansion the colours were more dominating with heart-shaped beds of purple 'Hidcote' lavender. And there is a long gravel walk punctuated at the sides by Versailles *caissons*, filled with flowers.

More roses fill a small formal garden, centred by a graceful arbour. But the garden was not all summer roses: Lord Haddington had a special penchant for heaths and heathers of all kinds and these with rhododendrons and azaleas occupied another area. Then there was an astonishing tunnel of apples heavily pruned, about a hundred years old. Finally there was the adaptation of a formal kitchen garden which Lady Haddington transformed into an area of great beauty using the old hedges and various formal features. This area, at the time of my visit, was decorated with splendid vases filled in a graceful way with the most elaborate planting I remember to have seen; silvery foliage accompanied the lavish though controlled flower colours, including large specimens of lavender-blue *Limonium arborescens*.

You need the best part of a day to savour all the controlled beauty at Tyninghame and glory in its manifold attractions through the year. It is not a garden to call and see in a hurry; the modern presentation of the whole is due to long hours of study and work and shows very fully what can be achieved in a given area by two people with similar tastes, and the ability to use them for the visitor's enchantment.

SIR HAROLD HILLIER

Ampfield House
ROMSEY • HAMPSHIRE
Hampshire County Council

THE GREAT NURSERY FIRM of Hillier and Sons had long been known to me through their informative catalogues and exhibits at Chelsea and other Royal Horticultural Society shows, but my first real contact was in about 1931. Being desirous of obtaining work in a nursery I had advertised my few assets — 'experienced in Botanic Garden and nursery' — in *The Gardener's Chronicle*. This brought a reply from Hillier's and I arranged to meet one of the firm at Chelsea. Who did this happen to be but Harold Hillier. We had a pleasant chat together and he was anxious for me to realize that I should, if I came to them, be just one of the ordinary staff. As it happened, I did not go to them, but accepted a position in a young wholesale firm near Woking, with good results.

Harold was of course a junior partner in the firm but had received exhaustive training in commercial horticulture in the parental firm and elsewhere, learning the very varied skills needed. Through the years and under his presidency the firm became much larger, not only on the chalk soil on which it started, but also on the lime-free soils to the south.

I came across Harold more and more frequently as the years rolled by. He was always kind and painstaking in his replies to one's queries. I remember particularly his little habit of turning over a leaf to examine the underside when asked for help in identification. He was a great asset on RHS Committee B, which dealt with trees and shrubs (and lilies) exhibited for possible awards, and of which I was also a member for some forty-five years. Many members were famous horticulturists, such as Tom Hay, the Hon. Lewis Palmer, Admiral Walker-Heneage-Vivian, Frank Knight, Lady Lawrence, Vera Higgins, Major Stern, and many more – including of course the redoubtable Edward Augustus Bowles the original instigator, and Norman H. Gould as secretary. Harold was always listened to with great attention when his rich voice proclaimed some important point of identification or cultivation.

But such are details in a remarkable life, which saw Hillier's nursery covering seven hundred acres and possessing the richest source of woody plants in the world, apart from Kew. It was not long before Harold's great drive led to the planting of a vast arboretum around their new headquarters, the historic Ampfield House, near Romsey. It was on very varied terrain and included a stream and lake as well as upland ground, and thus provided an ample range of sites and conditions for a major planting of, mainly, trees and shrubs. Some he brought as seed or propagating material from his trips abroad and others were garnered from the vast range of plants in British gardens. John Bond, serving his apprenticeship at Hillier's and later Keeper of the Savill Garden at Windsor, used to recall Harold with two or three helpers and a driver journeying with a lorryload of plants, instructing that they were to be planted where the roots fell. The result today is so beautiful and important that it has been taken into the capable hands of the Hampshire County Council and is open daily to the public. It includes Ampfield House, a scree garden, peat garden, pond and woodland and an avenue of magnolias. There are also two long borders mainly of shrubs but including herbaceous plants which were designed to commemorate the first one hundred years of Hillier's. Always a plantsman rather than a garden designer, he asked me how to keep up the interest of visitors to the long borders. I was then manager at Sunningdale Nursery where Jim Russell had planted two fairly long borders and was able to make the suggestion of a certain repetition of planting with something tall and striking.

Thus Harold not only was the great nurseryman but also the creator of many acres of land stocked with a huge collection of plants growing to maturity. It is an object lesson in what and how to plant and where, which his widow and sons, John and Robert, revere. So do we all. Harold was one of the very few men to have been knighted for his expertise in horticulture.

CHRISTOPHER AND BETTY HUSSEY

Scotney Castle
LAMBERHURST • KENT
National Trust

SET IN IDYLLIC SURROUNDS the property at Scotney awakens dreams – dreams of beauty recognized and used and also developed and built upon. There has been a dwelling here for eight hundred years; the great tower is the only one left of a castle built in the late fourteenth century within its moat. This tower, with its machicolations, was capped by a conical roof in the early eighteenth century. The property passed through three owners, being purchased by a Hussey in 1778.

I had long been captivated by the pictures of Scotney and wrote to Christopher Hussey some forty years ago requesting that I might come and see it all. I received a courteous reply and invitation and arrived on a lovely morning. The entry to the garden was by the large stone house – the stone came from a quarry on the slope below. From there across lawns we came to the Bastion or viewing point, devised by William Sawrey Gilpin a century or so earlier.

It was a wonderful stopping place, for there below, serene in its surrounding moat, was the castle tower and the remnants of old buildings. Fortunately Christopher Hussey appreciated all this, being an architectural historian, and spent all his later years in beautifying the view. He and his wife, Betty, used the existing *Rhododendron ponticum* which grew in monster clumps – and whose soft mauve flowers in June blend so happily with the fresh verdure of native trees – to act as a foundation in shape and colour for the planting of bold masses of scented azaleas and other shrubs, including kalmias for a long season of beauty. Since they are preceded by many spring bulbs elsewhere, and followed by blue hydrangeas, fuchsias and willow gentians and eventually plentiful autumn colour, the garden effect is well covered.

But I think it was not so much the creation of a garden that inspired the Husseys. We had learned to look back to the Picturesque period in art, and it was never more expressly shown than in this delightful prospect at Scotney. The whole valley seems there especially to hold in its hands the old building in its watery surround. It is an eye-opener as to what can be achieved with few elements. We walked all around and I came away enthralled – as I have been on subsequent visits.

Few people own so many separate attractions in their dwellings, nor can many show you the quarry whence the building stone came. And unique I think it is to have the imprint of an iguanodon's foot in what was mud some millions of years ago. How fortunate for us all it is that the whole place was given to the National Trust.

COLLINGWOOD ('CHERRY') INGRAM

BENENDEN • KENT
Privately owned

WHEN I WAS QUITE YOUNG we used to glory in the almond and prunus blossom in early spring followed by the pink thorn trees and the laburnums. They were everywhere. The flowering cherries had not arrived and although a few were known they were not popularized until Captain Ingram started collecting them, for which purpose he made many visits to Japan. They are overwhelmingly the most conspicuous in flower of all spring-flowering trees. Ingram procured propagating wood off several dozen varieties famous in Japan and had them grafted at the nursery of John Waterer, Sons and Crisp at Bagshot, Surrey.

For some fifty years they – or a few of them – have become popular in gardens, but their popularity over the last quarter century has been rather on the decline. This is for several reasons. First the normal understock for propagation is our native common cherry, *Prunus avium*; this is too strong for many of the varieties and renders them unsuitable for planting on lawns where the main supporting roots grow just below the surface and heave up the turf. One of the most unfortunate of practices is to graft them on to stems of *Prunus avium*, with the result that the appearance is highly artificial; the stems grow big and strong and thick making the heads quite incongruous. But if grown from cuttings the majority of varieties would remain as shrubs.

My interest in the Japanese cherries was awakened in the early 1930s; our nursery foreman, Arthur Gearing, had been taught his craft at Waterer's nursery and had introduced me to the beauty of these trees. Usually the first weekend in May saw them at their best; now it would probably be the last week of April, owing to the softening of the climate which has been going on since the nineteenth century. 'Kanzan' acts as a sort of timepiece. It is the most spectacular of the lot while young. Waterer's had made a show planting of them at Bagshot, and we used to go over on the first Sunday in May to revel in the established trees.

When cars became available to us we ventured to Benenden where 'Cherry' Ingram lived and had a good garden in which the cherries he had introduced played a large part. Fortunately he has set down for us all his findings about the *Sato Zakura* in his book *Ornamental Cherries* (1948), exquisitely illustrated by his own watercolours. But it was nothing short of a great treat to go to his garden where dozens of varieties were in flower and to be told all about them in his interesting way. And the cherries made life so good for rhododendrons, giving them just the right amount of shade.

Cherry had by no means a one-track mind, as his other book, *A Garden of Memories*, shows. I do not think I have ever met anyone with a more lively mind, twinkling eyes and engaging manner. He always entertained us in a deeply personal way. From one subject to the next, as in his book, he held forth and made foreign scenes appear to be next door. He had travelled widely over the world and frequently brought plants or seeds back to grow in his garden on the good loam of the Weald.

My remarks above should not convey to the reader that his garden was a jumble of plants. One of his maxims was that cherries and other trees and shrubs should shape the grass glades and always lead the visitor on, round a corner, to a fresh glade. This he did most successfully.

He was a great hybridist among rhododendrons, hardy gladioli and numerous other plants which he grew so successfully. The garden was always in good order, like his brain. There have not been many brains during the last century which could stand comparison with his. Besides the skill required in making a good garden he had a love of beauty and an accurate memory for plants and people, and where they came from and what they did.

THE EARL AND COUNTESS OF IVEAGH

Pyrford Court
WOKING • SURREY
Privately owned

SOMETIMES ONE NEGLECTS to visit often enough great gardens near at hand and yet will make much effort to see again and again those far away. This is how it was with me in regard to Pyrford Court, only a few miles away from Woking. In making their garden in the early 1930s Lord and Lady Iveagh became enamoured with the beauty of wisterias.

Wisterias are natives of the Far East and at the time of the Iveaghs they would have been provided by the Yokohama Nursery Company, which had a depot at St Albans, or from Gauntlett's of Chiddingfold. Pyrford Court is a ravishing sight at the time of their flowering for they cover the house in every colour between white, pink and purple. There was also a pergola covered with them.

Apart from this spring glory, Pyrford Court was noted for its gold and silver borders; Lady Iveagh was not only a friend and admirer of Gertrude Jekyll but was a woman of much taste in all things and with a good eye for colour. Both the borders were carried out mainly with evergreen shrubs and plants and were something quite new at the time; moreover I doubt if they have ever been repeated anywhere. There is a chance here for an enterprising young gardener! In their time I think they helped us to value leaves as much as flowers in creating schemes of colour. There is no doubt that the appreciation of leaves has grown much during successive decades.

THE HONOURABLE ROBERT JAMES

St Nicholas
RICHMOND • YORKSHIRE
Privately owned

I HAD HEARD A LOT about Bobbie James of Richmond in my early gardening days. He sat on the same committee of the Royal Horticultural Society as did F.G. Preston, the Superintendent of the Cambridge University Botanic Garden (where I was a student in the 1920s). The news of him that reached me made me long to see his garden. Alas! the opportunity did not occur until about 1950 when I made a tour of northern gardens in search of old roses. He had a large old house facing north or east in an elevated position at Richmond. I was amazed when I heard he did not own the house; however he purchased it later. He was closely in touch with the Royal Botanic Garden at Edinburgh and his garden was of such standing that there were occasional instances when young gardeners went from one to the other garden in search of greater experience. His property was called St Nicholas.

I soon found out from several visits that he was a born gardener and up to all manner of tricks to make rather tender plants thrive, such as deep mulches applied in autumn (often made from cut-down herbaceous plants, sawdust, and various hedge clippings, old manure with plenty of straw, spent hops and suchlike). Richmond is by no means a warm place but Bobbie loved to astonish his visitors in summer by having on display seemingly established plants of tender things such as *Salvia microphylla*, agapanthus and various South African daisies. The secret (only revealed to the few) was that he had a large greenhouse barely heated – just enough to keep out the frost. At the approach of autumn these tender plants were dug up and planted in the greenhouse and only watered once; by the end of May or early June they were again dug up and planted with almost immediate effect in the borders. They took a few weeks to present a good appearance.

Throughout the garden close attention was paid to colour effects as well as rare plants. He spent many years perfecting his own strain of sweet Williams – very dark reds and murrey tints – and loved the darkest roses of Gallica persuasion, dark hollyhocks and the like. It was when pastel shades and white gardens were coming into favour. He remarked to me that these pale colours were all very well but needed the reinforcement of dark reds and purples otherwise 'the borders look a bit thin'. I think he was right. Had it been available he would undoubtedly have grown *Cosmos atrosanguineus*, that lovely plant that smells like and approaches the colour of chocolate.

Not to be beaten by natives of California he tried the more hardy ceanothus, and I remember a very large bush of *Ceanothus thyrsiflorus* growing without protection. Many rare shrubs and plants decorated the garden which was given mainly to formal design, intriguingly different.

Among the many old roses he grew were two which I accepted with delight. They were the wild *Rosa gallica*, a single pink only a foot high, and the plant we used to call 'Empress Josephine' [now known as *R. x francofurtana*]. The legend has it that it was brought to England by the émigrés escaping the Revolution. Somehow it got into the hands of Ellen Willmott, who gardened so successfully at Great Warley in Essex (see page

Rosa 'Bobbie James'

244), and she passed it on to Bobbie. It is an obscure hybrid probably related to *Rosa cinnamomea*, judging by its foliage and scarcity of prickles. The flowers are as good as any Gallica variety but rather lacking in scent.

Bobbie and his wife, Lady Serena, were always very kind and hospitable and I treasure many memories. After he had died I called once and Lady Serena welcomed me. She was no gardener and spent the late years of her life playing bridge. We walked up and around the borders and as I was carrying (as usual) a camera I asked if I might take a photograph of one of the main borders. 'Do, by all means,' she said; 'where would you like me to stand?'

SIR JOHN JARVIS

Hascombe Court
GODALMING • SURREY
Privately owned

MANY YEARS HAVE PASSED since I paid my two visits to Hascombe Court, a noble half-timbered house of Sir Edwin Lutyens's design near Godalming in Surrey. It was all inspired by Sir John's desire for beauty and well did Sir Edwin marry all the disparate elements of the garden together. They were linked to the house by a large paved formal garden, entered by a splendid flight of broad steps. In the walls and paving there were many small and colourful plants including aubrietas, for it was spring and daffodil time. These were planted in their thousands and carried the eye in sheet after sheet of yellow and white with, less frequently, some orange-cup varieties. I have never seen such a lavish spread, even rivalling those in The Backs at Cambridge.

My second visit was in full summer to see the renowned herbaceous borders. Both visits were in the 1930s when gardeners were still employed in large numbers, a legacy from Edwardian days. The borders were therefore immaculately tended and full of varied colour in carefully graded heights. They were really good but were not in graded colours as Jekyll would have preferred.

The two visits brought home to me the splendour of the craft and art of gardening at that time. To my regret I never met Sir John but pen these few words to remind us of his success in blending trees and shrubs, bulbs and perennials, and a large rock garden into a joyous and beauty-laden home.

GERTRUDE JEKYLL

Munstead Wood
GODALMING • SURREY
Sir Robert and Lady Clarke

WHILE STUDYING THE CRAFT and science of horticulture in my early days in the late 1920s, I had also been captivated by the art. A friend lent me Gertrude Jekyll's *Colour Schemes for the Flower Garden* (1914), which fired my enthusiasm for graded colours in herbaceous borders.

On coming to work in Chobham, near Woking in Surrey, in June 1931, I lost little time before I managed to get permission to visit her renowned garden. And so, on a warm Saturday afternoon, 6 September, I cycled all the way through Guildford and Godalming to Munstead. There was only a handgate to her modest and charming home amongst the trees on the sandy rising ground. She received me sitting placidly in a chair, welcomed me and told me to walk around the garden, pick a piece of anything I wished to talk about and come back to the house for tea. My notebook reminds me of graceful bushes of *Leucothoë fontanesiana* (*L. axillaris*) and huge hummocks of *Gaultheria shallon*, with neither of which I was familiar, and a carpet of *Cornus canadensis* just coming into berry. Having been brought up in limy Cambridge I particularly remember these, and huge banks of azaleas and rhododendrons, kept well apart.

But it was the colour borders which enthralled me. I had never seen anything like them before, although I was a little prepared, in my imagination, by her writings. Since it was rather late in the summer, they were probably past their best, but a succession of colour was kept going by the expedient of putting in late-flowering plants grown in pots to prolong the season. The main flower border was a grand size, some 200 feet long by 14 feet wide, though reduced somewhat for planting by the shrubs at the back against the stone wall. Some of the shrubs augmented the colour scheming; others provided interest earlier in the year, for this big border was developed mainly to give colour through July until late September. I saw the Michaelmas daisy border that took over after the main border, and those leading to the Hut where she pursued her crafts. What was so remarkable about the colouring in the main border – from cool to strong and to cool again at the far end – was the solidity of the whole, bolstered by the shrubs and great clumps of *Yucca recurvifolia* and *Bergenia cordifolia* 'Purpurea'. I have not forgotten the wafts of scent from *Lilium auratum* and also the delicate pink *L. japonicum* (syn. *L. krameri*) and *L. longiflorum.* Golden privet, African marigolds, silvery *Brachyglottis* (syn. *Senecio*) and *Santolina* were all there contributing their bit; likewise cannas and dahlias. At the back was a group of the dignified *Helianthus salicifolius* (syn. *H. orgyalis*) not yet in flower; it looked like some burgeoning lily. This I took indoors to ask about.

The much narrower pair of borders along the path leading to the Hut was about at its best. The gorgeous red, yellow and orange tones 'hit' one and caused the eye to fly along them, coming to rest where the path was cleverly deflected to the left between hedge buttresses, the more easily to take in the change to silvery grey foliage and cool colours, contrasted by the sober dark green of fig, and bright blue of *Delphinium* 'Blue Fairy'. Another plant I picked to discuss with Miss Jekyll was the rare *Ophiopogon jaburan*, which I learned was pot-grown and plunged in position where an annual plant had spent itself.

Then there were cool, damp positions graced by the new lemon-yellow *Primula florindae* and contrasting blue trumpets of *Gentiana asclepiadea*. And, of course, a combination of frailty with firmness, a froth of *Aster divaricatus* (syn. *A. corymbosus*) draping over *Bergenia* leaves, a little feature I have often repeated. In those days hostas were practically unknown in gardens; at Munstead Wood one came across them grouped with ferns, and also standing in pots by one of the water tanks.

And so, in to tea. Miss Jekyll was still seated in the same chair, looking very like the portrait by William Nicholson, painted eleven years previously, her hair neatly parted in the middle. We examined my few specimens and I think she was rather surprised at how few there were. But though her garden was fully stocked it was at the time of summer flowers; well-tried plants, not rarities. In fact I had brought with me a few photographs, in monochrome, including that of *Lilium cernuum* and *L. nobilissimum* (syn. *L. alexandrae*) which I had in my garden at Cambridge, and I felt she did not take much interest in them! But in after years I realized not only that her sight was poor – through those tiny spectacles – but that her interest was in plants that made *effect* in gardens, not botanical rarities. She had after all been making her garden pictures for forty years, and had assessed and assimilated all the salient points and uses of every plant she grew.

Our tea was brought and we had it on occasional tables near the sunny windows; thin white bread and butter and a preserve (I do not remember what) and some little cakes. Her mellow voice floated on through the words of wisdom she imparted about my samples, and I came away deeply moved by all I had seen and heard. It was a pleasurable visit, long anticipated, and a lucky one for me, because she died in 1932. William Robinson, her famous gardening contemporary, went to her funeral. We all have profited almost unbelievably from their examples and written words; most of what we do in our gardens today stems from their ideas.

SIR GEOFFREY AND SUSAN
JELLICOE AND JOHN HUMPHRIS

Sutton Place
GUILDFORD • SURREY
Sutton Place Foundation

SUTTON PLACE is one of the finest old unfortified manor houses in the country, built in the early 1500s on a gift of land from Henry VIII to Sir Richard Weston. His descendants lived there for about three hundred years. Thereafter it had several owners. In the early twentieth century there was Lord Northcliffe, followed by the Duke of Sutherland, then J. Paul Getty. From 1976 to 1980 it served as the headquarters and offices of the Getty Oil Company. S.J. Seeger purchased it in 1980 and it is now owned by the Sutton Place Foundation. I have written all this to show that it has been lived in for all these years, but it needed repairing. This was organized by Frederick Koch and a more thorough reconditioning could hardly be imagined; I expect it is safe and sound for another four hundred years. Apart from lacking its imposing gatehouse and the fact that nothing is left of the original garden except for a few walls and a gazebo, it is, externally, the same as when Sir Richard Weston built it. During the early part of the twentieth century, Gertrude Jekyll added a few features to the garden.

Stanley Seeger, an American like Paul Getty, had the wit to get our great landscape artist, Sir Geoffrey Jellicoe, to rationalize and revamp what garden there was. It is extensive, covering in all sixty

acres, and sits on comparatively high land above a bend in the River
Wey south-west of Guildford, Surrey. Looking at it from a bird's-
eye point of view, it will be seen that the entrance to the house is
reached by a short avenue of American oaks. The view goes right
through the house and onwards to the south along a broad mown
path, guarded by Jekyllian obelisks of yew, to a large fountain
placed by the Sutton Place Foundation, while Jellicoe finalized the
northern end of the approach view with an immense lake. This
long walk might be called the stem of the cross for immediately
through the house there is a long, broad, east–west walk ennobled
by Jellicoe with paving, broken by two bosky hornbeam tunnels
and another gazebo, or, as it is called, the Gloriette, at the east end.

If we turn left on going through the house, along the south
walk, we enter two delightful gardens planted by Susan Jellicoe.
By the house and separated from it by a short moat is one of
Geoffrey's richest conceptions, the Paradise or East Walled
Garden. The patterned paths lead you past fountains whose
tinklings as well as birdsong enliven the air. The fountains are
lifted well above the ground and are enhanced by lofty hood-like
frames of slender ironwork, where in due season tall laburnums
drip their yellow racemes while climbing plants ascend. The
underplanting is rich and varied, mostly as designed by Susan.

Next is another formal area (the Moss Garden), dominated
by a great plane tree with moss established under it. The
surrounding borders are mostly in tones of purple and mauve
– Susan's choice – but the main work was organized by Patrick
Bowe for the Foundation.

The westerly end of the broad south walk passes the house
with its great magnolias and, in the lawn opposite, a very large
blue Atlantic cedar of unusual shape, covering its stem with
wide, flat skirts. But you will be tempted to enter what was the
original walled kitchen garden. Vegetables and flowers for

cutting are still grown here, but in addition to these attractions John Humphris, the head gardener for seventeen years, enriched the area with plants of all kinds — climbers on the walls and a glorious assortment of flowers and shrubs and several large rose beds. These roses and the old and new ramblers on the rose arcade, which bisects the garden, are all in pastel tints.

There are many other attractions on the way to a long formal pool designed with a Japanese touch. Beyond it, reflected in the water, is the huge slab of white Carrara marble to Ben Nicholson's design, which gives this part of the garden its name. There is much more yet to see; an open air theatre and extensive rose garden; a large plantation of named fruit trees, planted by the Foundation from 1988 onwards; in the grass beneath them are sheets of daffodils. And below, on ground sloping down to the river, is a notable and quite different planting. One might think one was in Cornwall for here are magnolias and other choice trees and shrubs and a splendid array of eastern Asiatic rhododendrons including some of the very large-leaved species, growing under scattered trees. It is a very relaxing part of the garden when that above it is so ordered and formal.

There is much more to see but I think I have written enough to indicate that this is a great garden, brought to a pitch of luxurious enjoyment in so many ways by Jellicoe and enhanced by sensitive and glorious planting, with a careful eye to colours. Very few gardens in the country have a finer selection of features. I have scarcely touched on Geoffrey's imagination, erudition and knowledge, brought forth to realize this fruit of his several years' work.

Now in the hands of the well-endowed Foundation, the attractions of the house and garden are likely to be well preserved. I always experience a mental uplift from a visit, at any time of year. Sir Geoffrey has brought all into focus and reason.

ARTHUR TYSILIO JOHNSON
AND NORA, HIS WIFE

Bulkeley Mill
TY'N-Y-GROES • NORTH WALES
Privately owned

HAVING LIFTED THE LATCH of the small handgate in the low stone wall there was always a special pleasure when one walked down the sloping path to the back door of The Bungalow in the Conway Valley. Steeply up the tree-clad slope came the sound of the rushing brook, a sound which has always lived with me. Otherwise there was a silence broken only by the rustling leaves, birdsong and sheep on the distant hills, visible through the trees. The kettle would usually be singing on the hob and Mrs Johnson would call 'Sara' to fetch A.T.J. down from his eyrie above. For it was not really a bungalow; another handgate led along a sunny path to the front door and the main rooms of the house. Above were two small rooms and below, the kitchen, which gave comforting warmth even in chilly weather. The whole building was set into the steep bank.

A.T. Johnson was born in the vicinity and spent his early years as a schoolmaster teaching, I infer, English, the Classics and perhaps what was then called Scripture. But his love of English led him to writing at an early age, with a leaning towards outdoor pursuits, all connected with wildlife. These and some poems appeared in various journals of the day. After his first, disastrous, marriage he met Nora Meek in about 1907 and they lived in close harmony until he died in 1956. To these early years belong his little pocket book *In the Land of the Beautiful Trout*, in which his love of the Welsh countryside shines forth. Shortly after, using the pseudonym 'Draig Glas' ('Blue Dragon'), he wrote *The Perfidious Welshman*, which had its second impression in 1910. In spite of the pseudonym, the authorship leaked out and he and Nora spent a long vacation in California, getting to know much about the flora and fauna of that state.

Originally the little house had only the steep tree-clad slope as a garden, with a small area of flat, damp ground below, outlined by the curve of the mill-race from Bulkeley Mill a hundred yards or so away, up the valley. The steep bank was stony and rooty and sharply drained, but a surprising number of plants grew there thanks to the rainfall, which I judge to have been about forty inches. The bank faced west and though well covered and surrounded by trees – mostly oaks, with a few ash trees and alders along the streams – it was a windy garden. The slope was threaded by narrow footpaths and steps. In fact the water-rounded rocks served as edging and walling stones, paving and steps; there was no shortage, and they gave the garden great character. One of the most pleasing effects in gardens in Wales, and indeed in the north of England, is the grey gravel as opposed to the yellow Thames gravel so prevalent in the south. The grey is so much more in harmony with flowers and leaves. For some of their wider planting areas on the flat the Johnsons hit upon the idea of making their own stepping stones, in the following way. First some small areas of spare ground had two inches of soil removed. The bottoms of these level hollows were sprinkled with the local shingle or gravel (usually granite), and over this was spread about two inches of concrete. When set the resulting slabs were lifted and turned over so that the surface presented the gravel and would not get slippery in wet weather. I understand many of these slabs are still in place.

In 1927 A.T.J.'s first gardening book appeared – *A Garden in Wales*. A few years previously the Johnsons had taken in a considerable piece of flat meadow, beyond the mill-race but bounded on the far side by the stream itself. Here was new scope for gardening, and the lease it gave upon a wider choice of plants prompted the book. There was room for a grass glade fringed by magnolias, firs, birches, *Nothofagus* and shrubs; it inspired me greatly when I first saw it in 1935 and continued to inspire me for twenty years of visiting it in alternate years. Much of it was shaded but a few years later the opportunity arose to acquire about a third of an acre of open ground to the south, including a place for a garage. This area was largely given to perennials and shrubs and *Magnolia* x *veitchii*, which grew with great rapidity. By then his second garden book had appeared, *A Woodland Garden*. After the war the Johnsons purchased a slice of meadow leading to Bulkeley Mill itself, restored the Mill fit to be let as a small dwelling, and repaired the great wooden waterwheel so that its plash, plash added to the music of the stream. Thereafter the postal address was changed to Bulkeley Mill. The piece of land that came with it was gravelly and open and gave the opportunity to grow a number of old and species roses, among other plants. *The Mill Garden* appeared in 1949, extolling many new plants. This was A.T.J.'s last major book, but he was kept busy on lesser publications by the successful little magazine called *My Garden*, owned and edited by Theo. A. Stephens. All this writing was done, not without great effort I believe, in the little top room; it was here that he conjured up those winning phrases and deep thoughts which have enchanted all who have read his words. There was no telephone to distract his thoughts.

With much of his time given to writing and photography, it is obvious that Mrs Johnson was also a great and efficient gardener. There were in all about four acres, and in its heyday the garden was always in first-class condition. I saw it in different seasons from spring to autumn. A very handy man with walling, fencing, mowing and all such jobs was he whom A.T.J. called 'Prometheus' in his writings, who worked with them for some forty years, two days a week. I fancy that in view of his name he must have been good at keeping bonfires going even in that rather damp climate! There was also Maggie, a home helper. Until her sight weakened, Mrs Johnson did all the typing. It was a very happy working group and no time was wasted. His writing attracted visitors, who were not always welcome because of the time they absorbed, but they were always made to *feel* welcome. In a garden of that size, and run to such high standards, there were always pressing jobs to be done.

The Johnsons may be said to have grown with their garden. Their keen love of plants and avid desire for more and more of them as the total area grew meant visits to other gardens and nurseries, occasionally to the shows of the Royal Horticultural Society, and travels to Scotland and distant parts of England. Among their fast friends were Walter Ingwersen and W.J. Marchant, two nurserymen of great repute and kindness from whom many nuggets arrived. But they knew and were known by many of the leading horticulturists of the first half of the last century.

Both Ingwersen and Marchant were mostly occupied with and interested in the plants of the wild, the species, not the highly bred 'grandifloras' of the nursery and seed trades. These plants of refinement gave the garden its whole character. And character it truly had. I think the word 'gentle' sums it up as well as any. There were practically no straight lines or unnecessarily curving paths; all routes through the garden followed the contours, easily, gently, always leading one on to a fresh peep between shrubs up or down the valley. They also had an almost uncanny knack of placing plants, so that they would thrive and 'look comfortable'. There were no harsh orange or red colourings; the whole garden was filled with gentle tints from white to light yellow, clear and deep pinks, mauves and blues and dark purples, all backed by the native vegetation. The choice of colours was not always easy. To bolster his selection of plants for his writing A.T.J. needed great variety. Sometimes when tempted at a show or nursery he would be warned by Nora that 'such a colour would upset your nightingales' – or, I might have added, the willow warblers.

The garden owed as much to William Robinson as to Gertrude Jekyll; there were no herbaceous borders or graded colour schemes. It was perhaps the most important and original of what are called 'ecological' gardens today, where each plant's preferences were studied, bringing into things a wholeness and a gentleness new to the century. There is no doubt that his outpouring of articles and many books exercised a great influence in their day. They were all illustrated by his highly skilled photography, close-ups of plants in the main and without, unfortunately, many views. While he gloried in the shrubs and trees and woodland plants – the rhododendrons, *Ericaceae*, birches, cherries, conifers and bulbs – 'Herself' (or 'The Lady of the Garden'), as he would call her in his writings, treasured everything including tiny shrubs, primulas, meconopsis, and alpines. Thus there was an exceptionally wide range of plants from aconites to *Pieris nana* (syn. *Arcterica nana*), from rhododendrons and hellebores to eucryphias and

Nothofagus. And there was never a shortage of paths and views to be enjoyed, morning, afternoon or evening.

Perhaps after a long morning in the garden the weather would tempt a visit to nearby Bodnant – always a Mecca for gardeners – or the Happy Valley Gardens at Llandudno (full of good plants); or perhaps an expedition to Cemaes Bay on Anglesey where the dunes were blue with *Scilla verna*, or a trek over the hills to the Auld Brig. And home in the early evening chill which falls so quickly in those damp valleys as soon as the sun sinks behind the hills – home to the quickly kindled range and a high tea, and long discussions about plants and this and that.

I heard the history of their *Daphne cneorum* 'Eximia'; *D. cneorum* was a well-known plant before the Second World War and used to be on every rock garden at Chelsea, but it suddenly lost its vigour. The Johnsons bought a plant from J. Stormonth's nursery at Carlisle which had been collected in the wild, and raised seed from it, and the result was this now well-known and brilliant clone enjoyed by all gardeners who can grow it. There were two self-sown plants in the garden which have achieved equal fame: *Cytisus* 'Johnson's Crimson', of intense colouring, no doubt inheriting its crimson tint and small flowers from *C.* x *dallimorei* which grew near by. And the same was presumed about *Erica* x *darleyensis* 'Arthur Johnson', which might be described as a great improvement on the Darley Dale cross, with much longer flower spikes.

A booklet which A.T. Johnson wrote entitled *Labour-Saving Plants* summed up for the first time how plants can be used not only to beautify the garden but, by virtue of their ground-hugging propensities, to avoid the use of hoe or spade. There is no doubt that much of the success and beauty of his garden was due to the use of these plants. Not only did they cover the ground to the exclusion of weeds, but the carpets and clumps of foliage and flower made the perfect complement and contrast to the dominance of shrubs in the scheme of things. Even today some of his plantings, notably of epimediums, remain free of weeds. Among these plants none was accorded more praise than the hardy geraniums. I did not discover how the pale form of *Geranium pratense* cropped up, but it was a favourite in the garden, and caught the eye of Mr B. Ruys of the famous Moerheim Nursery in Holland, who begged for some seeds. These duly germinated and among them was a stranger, a splendid lavender-blue of short stature which was put on the market in 1950 as 'Johnson's Blue'. It was probably a hybrid of *G. himalayense*, and has achieved great fame. Two hybrids of *G. endressii* were *G. x oxonianum* 'Rose Clair' in salmon-pink and *G. x o.* 'A.T. Johnson' in pale silvery pink. They were listed by Ingwersen, as was *Mimulus* 'A.T. Johnson', a gorgeous seedling of wallflower red edged with yellow which he had found in a boggy stream in the hills. A journey by car to south-western Scotland produced the pure pink *Geranium sanguineum* 'Glenluce', a welcome change from the normal 'bloody cranesbills', and with extra-dark-green leaves. It is a favourite with lovers of lowly plants.

We owe to the Johnsons, I believe, the many tints of columbines from white to pink and plum colour and to blue, self-tinted or perhaps parti-coloured, on which they exercised their skills as selectors and improvers of the 'Hensol Harebell' strain, influenced by the old granny's bonnets of the Welsh cottage gardens. It is worth noting here that *Ceanothus* 'A.T. Johnson' was raised by Burkwood and Skipworth at Kingston upon Thames, and named in his honour. One winter they went to the Riviera and found in bloom in February a form of *Calluna vulgaris* which they brought back and called 'Hiemalis' – a useful plant seldom seen today.

I consider A.T.J.'s was the outstanding garden of its kind and size during the second quarter of the century. As the years passed and towards the end of the planters' lives it became overgrown, without skilled staff to keep it in order. But such is the fate of most personal gardens. Among the principles they observed, the most sacrosanct was 'the preservation of a garden atmosphere which shall be, as near as is humanly possible, in harmony with the wild's uncultured beauty'. Their garden achieved the nearest I have ever seen to this most difficult of all garden styles – that of being naturally beautiful and intriguing without ever being wild.

After Mrs Johnson's death Maggie and Prometheus married and lived at The Bungalow, which they called Oak Bank. Eventually Oak Bank and the Mill were sold, but I hear of the many fine specimen trees that still stand guard over the glade: *Aesculus* x *neglecta* 'Erythroblastos', *Cercidiphyllum*, *Koelreuteria*, magnolias, birches, *Abies*, *Davidia*, *Metasequoia*, *Athrotaxis*, *Nothofagus*, and many rhododendrons and good shrubs. The owners keep the lawns well mown and must greatly enjoy each year's unfolding beauty. And still the chattering stream flows down the gentle meadow slopes.

Facing west, set into an ivy-clad bank halfway up the slope, is a small stone seat. At its back is a slab of stone with the lettering 'In the garden of happy memories it is always summer'. So it is with me.

MAJOR LAWRENCE JOHNSTON

Hidcote Manor
CHIPPING CAMPDEN • GLOUCESTERSHIRE
National Trust

THE GARDEN AT HIDCOTE has been famous for many
years. It is not a garden of great size nor has it a
particularly long history as gardens go. The estate was
purchased some ninety years ago by Major Lawrence
Johnston, and with the aid of the existing farmhouse, a
few walls, a cedar of Lebanon, and five large beech
trees, he created with taste and courage a garden which
has become internationally famous. In general it may be
summed up as a garden on architectural lines, deriving
from Italy and France, with lavish and varied planting;
the planting has always been allowed, even encouraged,
to soften the firm lines of the design and to exhibit an
exuberance at all times. In detail, it is a series of gardens
each with a definite colour scheme. These separate areas
are divided by hedges and walls and are on an intimate
scale, whereas to provide complete relief there are two
very long narrow vistas extending into the countryside
and a splendid large open lawn.

The above paragraph is from my book *Gardens of the National Trust*.
The property was purchased in 1907 by Mrs Winthrop,
Johnston's mother, who wanted to encourage him to be a farmer.

Fortunately for us he became enthused with garden design and the example he left us has had a major influence on gardens in this country, and also abroad, during the last century. Unfortunately we know little about the development of the garden, which grew over the years with the addition of new features as dictated by the lie of the land. The garden was given to the National Trust in 1948. Johnston had begun to lose his memory and spent most of his later years at his other garden the Serre de la Madonne in the south of France. At one time there was in existence a 'garden book', a sort of diary I think which would give us much history, but it disappeared. [Some of it has recently been rediscovered.]

When the National Trust took over, the garden was very run down and gradually got worse because the head gardener, Frank Adams, had died and the staff took little notice of the propagator to whom the Gardens Committee gave instructions. There was therefore little to help me make decisions when the post of Gardens Adviser was created. The design was intact, however, and a number of beds and areas still had enough old plants in them to indicate what should be done.

I had fortunately been taken round the garden by the head gardener a few years before he died, and subsequently went round with Major Johnston. But it was too late. The planting had slipped too far and most of his old friends in the neighbourhood had also died. The result was that the rehabilitation of the planting was left to me and the members of the Gardens Committee. I used to pay a visit, usually for a day, in every other month of the year, and gradually the garden was brought up to exhibition standard by the energy and interest of the head gardener, G.H. [George Harry] Burrows, and the National Trust agent concerned, Colin Jones.

Johnston did not spend lavishly on the creation of the garden. Stone was easy to come by in the Cotswolds and he knew how to use it. He was always on the look-out for new plants for his garden.

There is no doubt that the garden is intriguing and captivating. It started around the house where there was a walled area and a few beds, a cedar of Lebanon, and a little stream which came under the wall and went downhill at an angle to the house. The hilly terrain gave many difficulties but Johnston solved them all — triumphantly. Witness the two major formal views: they are uplifting to the eye and the senses; they both go up slopes to infinite views, not to a statue or other commanding ornament. The main view from under the cedar in the old walled garden, through the gates and the rond-point, the grass path between the red borders, up the steps and between the gazebos, through the *palisades à l'Italienne* (the Stilt Garden), then through the great gates and into the countryside is undoubtedly a masterpiece of garden design. Then there is the relief of a noble lawn. This must have been levelled by Johnston, because there were huge old beeches at either end, those at the far end standing on raised ground, often called the theatre. Hedges abound, carving the spaces into 'rooms', each with its own view or, occasionally, a view into another hedged enclosure. In spite of the prevailing limy soil Johnston was desirous of growing rhododendrons and camellias; this was achieved by the liberal use of rotted sawdust and perhaps peat. (He may of course have discovered, as at nearby Kiftsgate Court and Sezincote, that there were veins of lime-free soil running along the slopes!)

He was also a planter of avenues, though the principal one sadly succumbed to elm disease in its fiftieth year; there is one of close-set beeches within the garden and a short one leading

Rosa 'Lawrence Johnston' (top right)
and *R.* 'Cupid'

approximately east from the house towards a statue. But I think I have written enough to call attention once again to all the mysteries, ingenuities and schemes which make this garden so irresistible. Those needing more details must refer to Ethne Clarke's excellent book *Hidcote, The Making of a Garden* (1989), or better still make some visits during the year which will reveal the deep understanding of design and the use of plants.

FRANK P. KNIGHT

Knap Hill Nursery
WOKING • SURREY
Knap Hill and Slocock Nurseries

Soon after i finished my training in gardening and botany in the University Botanic Garden at Cambridge, I mentioned to the Superintendent, Mr Preston, that I had secured a job in a nursery in the village of Chobham, near Woking in Surrey. To me it was a relief and an excitement to be moving to an acid soil where rhododendrons grew readily and hydrangeas were mainly blue. He announced that a friend of his, Frank Knight, had just been appointed manager of one of the several famous nurseries in the district, Knap Hill Nursery, and he kindly gave me a letter of introduction to Frank. Thus began a long friendship. I arrived at Chobham in June and lost no time in getting an invitation to meet Frank and see the nursery.

It was one of the oldest nurseries in the district, started in 1760. Whereas the area around Fulham had at one time a number of progressive nurseries, the land they took up became very valuable for building so near to London and they all gradually moved to Surrey where the soil was sandy and not popular for farming. At the same time, when horse power was extra popular – for ploughing and transport – it meant that trees and shrubs could easily be transported to London and other populous places, and loads of manure could be brought back. The Waterer family produced a string of famous names in the nursery world – John, Michael and Hosea, as well as Anthony who started Knap Hill. By the time I arrived in the district Anthony had gone and Lionel de Rothschild had purchased the nursery as well as much of the surrounding land, houses and cottages. He had installed R.C.H. Jenkinson and F. Gomer Waterer to run the nursery, with Frank Knight as nursery manager.

Frank had received some of his training at Kew where he became deeply interested in the propagation of rare trees and shrubs from cuttings. The most renowned quarterly magazine devoted to plants and gardens during the 1930s was *The New Flora and Silva*, published by Dulau and Co. of London and edited by E.H.M. Cox who gardened near Perth in Scotland. Several articles appeared from Frank's pen on the propagation of rare trees and shrubs.

The nursery had many outstanding trees, such as liquidambars over sixty feet high, a huge weeping *Sophora japonica* and an immense fern-leaved beech and a weeping beech. The last two are still standing. The weeping beech, whose original stem shows it was grafted, has some fifty subsidiary stems which have grown up from branches which had touched the ground and taken root. The area covered by this fantastic array of stems covers about an acre and the tallest stems achieve some fifty or sixty feet. It must be the largest tree of any kind in the

British Isles, though in girth and height is rivalled by the great plane at Mottisfont Abbey.

It was a real treat to have made friends with Frank and we had many enjoyable evenings together, going round the acres which long ago had been drained by interlocking ditches which provided irrigation during dry spells. Judging by the many specimens of great size to be found there, the soil is very fertile and deep, of what is known as Bracklesham Loam.

It was a wonderful establishment in the 1930s, during which years an outpost was started on the main road to Portsmouth and Southampton, in Hampshire. This was to catch customers travelling by car, for the nursery itself was on a by-road with no impressive frontage. Spreading its wings to the utmost the nursery also went in for perennial plants and I was commissioned to build a rock garden of some twenty tons of Westmorland limestone. This I did of an evening, picking up three able-bodied workmen *en route*. This all came under Frank's jurisdiction; he had worked for some years at Baker's nursery at Codsall near Wolverhampton, where the Russell lupins were first launched. Unhappily the rock garden was dismantled during the war.

Bobby Jenkinson, a keen plantsman, lived at Knaphill Manor, which could be reached by a mile-long drive through the nursery and fields, lined with rhododendrons. In a sheltered corner *Epigaea repens* thrived, making a patch several yards across. The rhododendrons were Gomer Waterer's special pride and joy and he continued raising new varieties, though I believe his own favourite was the old semi-double 'Fastuosum Flore Pleno', a cool lavender blue. His son Donald honoured me long after the war by naming after me a rich amethyst-lilac seedling of *R. campanulatum* raised by his father.

But the war came with disastrous effect. Frank was moved to the Camouflage Board and spent the next four years buying large specimen trees to help screen the various aerodromes and hangars about the country, and Donald Waterer joined the Royal Air Force and was twice severely wounded. He eventually returned to Knap Hill nursery. Frank meanwhile had become manager for R.C. Notcutt's famous nursery at Woodbridge, Suffolk. I had visited this nursery twice before the war in the company of Roger Notcutt, who sadly died early in life, and thus Mrs R.C. Notcutt was looking for someone to run the nursery. Frank spent some ten years there pulling it together and later became director of the Royal Horticultural Society's garden at Wisley, eventually retiring in good health after a rewarding life in gardening, with many honours and awards. We both served on Committee B for approximately fifty years. During all the years we had remained close friends and on one occasion at Woodbridge he took me to a large derelict area peopled almost entirely by very ancient oaks interspersed with birch and holly trees of immense height and girth. The legend went that William the Conqueror had rewarded one of his faithful followers with the land, with permission to take one crop off it. The recipient sowed acorns ...

MAJOR AND MRS KNOX FINLAY

Keillour Castle
PERTHSHIRE • SCOTLAND
Privately owned

THESE POTENTIALLY FAMOUS garden and plant lovers purchased the Keillour estate in 1938 and spent the rest of their lives in creating and developing a wonderful garden. They had a most beautiful, semi-wooded area as a backcloth with deep valleys containing two burns and yet the castle, built in 1887, stands in a commanding position with the upland parts of the garden around it. It is not on record where the new owners acquired their skill and knowledge of gardening, but the terrain, with its hills and burns, and great trees thriving in the lime-free soil presumably led them on. There is no doubt that they gave us a unique garden packed with trees, shrubs and plants of amazing diversity which would be hard to equal. They lived just at the time when many of the plants from eastern Asia were crowding our gardens and they undoubtedly found conditions to their liking at Keillour – in fact Sir George Taylor claimed that the conditions at Keillour were 'strongly reminiscent of the gorge country of south-east Tibet'. Small wonder was it that the new owners were led on by all the new discoveries from that part of the world, and elsewhere.

The Knox Finlays used to tantalize us in the Royal Horticultural Society when, almost every year, they brought specimens of their treasures to the shows and almost always captured an award or two. Long before the present craze for hellebores started I remember their showing some superbly coloured, sized and shaped seedlings. Rare lilies, *Meconopsis*, primulas of the *Petiolaris* and other sections, and many other delicate flowers survived the long journey down from Scotland, to appear fresh on the morrow at the show.

It was a particular pleasure being welcomed by them on a lovely day in July and being taken round the many acres of garden and finally being given tea – or lunch – on one of the few flat lawns with rare and beautiful plants on every side. A few years later I went again, sadly after the Major had died, specially to study the various species and hybrids of *Meconopsis*. It was the occasion when I saw *M.* x *sarsonsii* in creamy white at its best, *Nomocharis* species, *Diphylleia cymosa*, incarvilleas and *Lilium ciliatum*.

The approach to the castle takes you over a graceful bridge spanning the deep valley with the hurrying Horn burn at the bottom. No doubt this moving water did much to carry away the cold air at the bottom of the valley when frosts threatened. At all events the steep sides of the valley – with thick or scattered trees, rare *Abies* and *Picea* and magnolias included – made perfect homes for rhododendrons of all kinds, from miniatures to giants with leaves as much as three feet long; and tucked away were gentians, the willow gentian among them, *Kirengeshoma* and more kinds of *Meconopsis*. It was a wonderland only equalled – scarcely surpassed – by the Royal Botanic Garden at Edinburgh.

THE MARCHIONESS OF LONDONDERRY

Mount Stewart
NEWTOWNARDS • CO. DOWN • NORTHERN IRELAND
National Trust

THE SIXTH MARQUESS OF LONDONDERRY inherited Mount Stewart during or soon after the Great War. There was I suppose some semblance of a garden but Lady Londonderry's impression was simply of two immense Irish yews very near to the south windows of the house. She had been brought up in a great house and garden in Scotland, Dunrobin Castle, so gardening was 'in her blood', so to speak, and she was of a bold mind, hence what she did with such verve and knowledge at Mount Stewart from 1921. She had a free hand and ample means.

The front court is surrounded by a low wall; above are conical bay trees which, like other much larger ones on the west front of the house, were imported, fully matured, from Belgium in 1923. Going through the house one comes out under a portico on the south front. Her great parterre is devoted to two patterns of beds, each with a central pool and fountains but with different colour schemes. All around are effigies of birds and animals made of *ciment-fondu*. At first sight these strike a whimsical note, but many of them represent the animals adopted as classless nicknames for Lord Londonderry's colleagues in the services in the Great War. Down a large flight of steps is the Spanish House with blue-green tiles. Here the

Fuchsia 'Mount Stewart'

colour scheme is again different, with tree peonies and glaucous foliage. From there you can enter the Lily Wood, an area full of treasures. The Mairi Garden is towards the east, planted in blue and white, with 'silver bells' (campanulas) and cockle shells, but not 'all in a row'!

On the other hand, going west from the house there is the Sunk Garden, with a pergola above the walls covered with lovely climbing plants in strong blue and yellow and orange and four large beds of perennial plants in the same colours. But in early summer the whole area is dominated by a massed array of the orange azalea 'Coccineum Speciosum'. Up steps and we enter the

Shamrock Garden, hedged around with yew and containing not only a rich collection of plants but the Red Hand of the O'Neill.

In tribute to her mother's imaginative skills in design, her daughter, Lady Mairi Bury, created a further vista leading away westwards, with embothriums, white lilacs, orange-cupped narcissi and purple hydrangeas.

But so far we have recalled only the formal gardens. Leading from the front portico are broad paths, richly planted with shrubs and trees to take you to the lake, around which are more and more lovely things, all culminating in *Tir na nóg*, the family burial ground – the 'Land of the Ever Young'. And then away to the Jubilee Glade with its eucalyptus trees and the model of a white stag and back to the mansion through great trees.

What I have written is just a general survey from memory of a truly great garden – one of the very finest in the British Isles. The whole area echoes Lady Londonderry's remarkable achievement. And not only was she able at garden design but she was also a plantswoman of great knowledge. Wherever you go you may be sure to find some plant that you have never seen before, from the southern as well as the northern hemisphere. *Davidia*, *Weinmannia trichosperma*, rhododendrons of all sorts, many of them tender and also scented; *Picconia*, *Prostanthera*, *Bowkeria*, *Psoralea*, *Clianthus*, *Erica canaliculata*, pittosporums, *Magnolia* x *wieseneri* (syn. *M.* x *watsonii*), *Wisteria brachybotrys* 'Shiro-kapitan' (syn. *W. venusta*), *Kniphofia snowdenii*, *Myosotidium hortensia*, *Stenanthium robustum*, *Boenninghausenia albiflora*, *Acca* (syn. *Feijoa*) and grevilleas, and of course *Eucalyptus* species which so faithfully scent the air. There is also on warm days the lovely strawberry scent of the Douglas firs which shelter the garden.

Much of it had 'slipped' during the Second World War but fortunately Nigel Marshall, the head gardener, rose to the occasion and brought it back to its magnificence.

My first visit was long ago and I remember well how impressed I was with the ordered colours, apart from the design. The azaleas were at their best. After Lady Londonderry's death the mansion and garden passed to the National Trust and I made at least two visits a year, in different months, and got to know a lot of the tender shrubs which so enrich the garden. It was wonderful to wake up in the great house and feel the joys of the impressive garden all around. Few people have so great a monument – all created by one brain in a lifetime.

VERA MACKIE

Guincho

NEAR BELFAST • CO. DOWN • NORTHERN IRELAND

Privately owned

AFTER SEVERAL INVITATIONS I managed to visit Guincho, the home and garden of Vera Mackie and her husband. The sun shone on us and on the house, which had a character derived from architecture in Portugal or southern Spain, and stood on what is always a gardener's dream – good soil and varied terrain. Vera had catholic tastes, a vast knowledge of plants and fortunately she not only knew how to grow them but she also had the ability to display them well. In its heyday no garden in Ireland was more loved or more full of treasures in herbaceous plants. There was a substantial flat lawn with beds of Gallica and other old roses embroidered with alchemilla and a low retaining wall stocked with all manner of rock plants.

I remember a visit by the International Dendrology Society, of which Vera and I were both members, to the Botanic Garden at Cambridge. After a brief general look round, Vera went to the botanical order beds to see whether there was anything to augment her own collection. It is not perhaps surprising that there was nothing she coveted. Her own was so rich in moisture, sunshine, shade and all the necessaries that go to make a perfect garden, that she could always find a spot to suit the most difficult or demanding of plants. Her garden was much filled with perennials, interspersed with spring and autumn bulbs, and certain shrubs. There was always something beautiful to see. At one point there was a steep bank – almost vertical – above a shady moist patch; the bank supported the largest clumps I have ever seen of the lovely native fern *Polystichum setiferum*, and brought home to one that the numerous crested and plumose variants which the nineteenth-century gardeners fancied had no greater attraction than the wild species when well grown.

And this is what Vera's forte was – to know and grow to perfection all the plants in her garden. Moist patches had rodgersias and veratrums; dry sunny areas disported alstroemerias and rare silver-leaved *Senecio doronicum*; shady spots were given to trilliums and erythroniums; in between, in the more normal positions were hosts of plants that few gardeners could name. Sadly she died in her full experience and ability, but her head gardener tended her plants for several years under the new ownership. Nothing was ordinary at Guincho; the garden of two to three acres sparkled with rarities, all well grown. Beauty adorned it in the century's middle decades and her cuisine was delectable, likewise.

L. MAURICE MASON

Talbot Manor
KING'S LYNN • NORFOLK

IT WAS A LOVELY SUNNY AFTERNOON when my old friend George Crosbie Taylor took me to Talbot Manor to meet Maurice Mason and his wife, Margaret. We spent several hours going round the well-stocked garden and it was obvious that Maurice was not only a fair size himself but also had a large brain. He was a skilled and able farmer. He knew every plant in the garden by its Latin name whether it was a tree, shrub or diminutive plant, both out of doors and in his extensive glasshouses. These I think became his first love, as he had land in Southern Rhodesia, and got to know a vast number of the native plants. In addition to which he had become friends with Herbert Whitley who ran the Primley Zoo at Torquay, where plants were almost as prized as animals. I remember on my one and only visit to the zoo how impressed I was with the great number of exotic species, all so carefully grown. Every winter Maurice and Margaret journeyed to somewhere in the warm south – New Guinea, Madagascar, Costa Rica and many places in South America – always bringing back plants which appealed to him.

But it must not be thought that this was all for vainglory. On the contrary, Maurice did a very great deal to interest and influence the public. Apart from gaining awards and certificates at the Royal Horticultural Society shows, he and his devoted gardening staff showed great groups of greenhouse and other plants for about thirty-five years at the Chelsea Show, achieving a long succession of gold medals. His collection of plants was so large that many botanic gardens in Europe benefited by his gifts and twice he exhibited at the Ghent Floralies, at one of which his 'Iron Cross' *Begonia* achieved the award for the best new plant, eventually being named *B. masoniana.*

In the meanwhile the garden at Talbot Manor prospered and was enlarged. At one time he set aside a large, long new border at the back of the manor and asked me to fill it with as large a collection of variegated shrubs and plants as possible. Although we had met first several years previously, one of the ways he showed his kindly friendship was by sending me substantial orders to Sunningdale Nursery where I had become manager.

But in 1972 the price of oil went up so considerably that what had started as an enjoyable hobby became a heavy liability and as a result tropical plants were 'out' and the greenhouses became filled with plants which would have been classed as scarcely hardy in cold Norfolk. He had purchased some years before what became known as Larchwood a few miles away, in the midst of which he had a small bungalow. This was enlarged in due course and, now that greenhouse work had become so limited, the acres of young larches made a good setting for extensive new plantings of hardy trees and shrubs. Ambitiously and with great interest he started a collection of rhododendrons and allied shrubs, but they were all killed in an extra cold winter. Such is the enormous variety of natives of cold and temperate parts of the world that this did not deter him. He was always planting new things and what is more could always tell you where they came from as well as their Latin names.

Sadly, for the last three years of his life he was confined to a wheelchair, but still visited Chelsea and other shows and botanic and other interesting collections of plants as far away as Edinburgh. There is one thing more I must mention before I close this little essay, and that was that he never forgot he was planting beautiful things and always contrived to make them appear naturally placed and grouped to embellish his ground. It is a pity that so many of the botanically minded, or over-rich, did not do the same. I look back on many happy times at his homes and found his wife, Margaret, a keen disciple in gardening and a splendid hostess. His youngest son Hugh has some of his wonderful enthusiasm for plants.

Maurice went through horticulture like an express train; few could keep up with him.

BERNARD MAXWELL

Steadstone
DALBEATTIE • KIRKCUDBRIGHTSHIRE • SCOTLAND

HAVING STAYED WITH CUBBY ACLAND (see page 62), the National Trust's regional agent for Cumbria, on many occasions when my duties took me that way, we decided, one autumn, that the next year we would make a tour of certain Scottish gardens. Accordingly we set off on a gloomy June morning in the late 1970s when it was pouring heavily with rain to go to Steadstone. It was Cubby's choice; I had not heard of it. The rain eased as we approached our goal, which was a modest little house perched on a hillock in a very rocky and delightsome district. The sun came out suddenly and by the time we had been welcomed and went out the garden door the brilliance of the day was upon us, intensified by the clean, washed air.

I shall never forget that first view of the garden. It would perhaps be better to describe it as planted landscape, dominated by an enormous outcrop of grey stone some sixty feet high, shapely and cut into various sections. It stood isolated in a grassy valley, decorated with a few native birch trees and surrounded by scattered woodland. In the foreground were the arching branches of an old thorn tree, covered with white bloom, and down below, on the sward, the remains of walls round an old pigsty, neither of which we had come to see!

Bernard Maxwell had been very skilful over many years in planting exotic shrubs and plants wherever there was sufficient soil to give them root-hold, and he had done it all with due attention to the astonishing lump of rock and the delicate tracery of the few birch trees. The photograph I took that day is reproduced in my *The Art of Planting* and well did it deserve to be shown.

We were of course very lucky in the brilliance of the day, which showed up everything to perfection. The most commanding plants were two *Viburnum plicatum* 'Mariesii' covered with bloom and like white tablecloths. Winding footpaths of grey gravel took us between the widely grouped shrubs across the rough-mown meadow. Clumps of native ferns and hostas acted as a foil to cut-leaved Japanese maples. The placing of azaleas of all sorts had been carefully managed so that there was not a surfeit of them anywhere.

Apart from the imposing block of grey rock there was below it a small stream in the grassy slopes, while above the main block on the other side there was a small upward glen likewise gently planted, which made one realize that the great outcrop of rock was merely the face of a vast eminence.

I was only able to visit Steadstone once, to my regret, but I saw signs of summer colour from spreads of astilbes in the moister parts – though the area is blessed with ample rainfall – and also several of the greater hydrangeas with their velvety leaves. They would have been a great sight.

Bernard kindly followed up our visit with a photograph taken on 20 October 1980, which showed that his artistic planting was as much for effect late in the year as in its early summer glory and freshness. The azaleas and maples were transformed into widely separated clumps of fiery colours – scarlet, orange, yellow and the subdued russet tints that go with them.

In all the visit was an eye-opener, showing how one could enjoy all the exotic treasures that we have accumulated from around the world, without losing the beauty of the native scenery. I hope some of the many visitors who must have gone to Steadstone have done something like it in their respective homes.

SIR HERBERT EUSTACE MAXWELL

Monreith
WIGTOWNSHIRE • SCOTLAND
Privately owned

MY FIRST INTIMATION of the work of this great gardener came through his contributions of articles and watercolours of some choice plants in *The New Flora and Silva*, in the late 1930s. Thereafter I acquired his two fine books: *Trees, A Woodland Notebook* (1915), and *Flowers, A Garden Notebook* (1923). These were acquired second-hand, long after the print had run out. Beauty has always been a goal for me and here were two books written with charm and erudition which gave great delight. The former is illustrated with a rare selection of well-reproduced photographs in colour and black-and-white; the latter enjoys a dozen lovely watercolours by the author.

The gentle, rambling, but highly informative writing leads one from page to page and chapter to chapter. He was obviously a friendly soul since numerous famous gardeners are mentioned in each book – throughout the British Isles and also in other countries.

The mild climate of Wigtownshire enabled him to grow many somewhat tender shrubs and plants, on lime-free soil. Thus he was able to embrace rhododendrons and other shrubs with the same preferences. I believe it was a spacious garden surrounding a great house and can imagine the garden to have been not only well stocked, but planted with understanding. It is obvious from his writings that he was deeply steeped in history and the classics as well as botany and forestry. But he was above all I think a great gardener.

He loved all plants except voracious spreaders – having been led astray by *Persciaria sachalinensis* (syn. *Polygonum sachalinense*); early in the book is a sentence which I think underlies all that he wrote: 'The intrinsic beauty of a plant is not enhanced by its rarity or novelty.' Here we have one of the great home truths which we should all do well to heed. It is elaborated in a charming aside which Sir Herbert relates in some detail:

> One day in early May, 1913, the late Mr Joseph Choate, so long and affectionately esteemed as American Ambassador at St James's, drove me in his car across Long Island to lunch with Theodore Roosevelt at Sagamore

Hill. The woods through which lay our route were full of *Cornus florida*, loaded with white – on some bushes with bright rose-blossom.

'What a splendid thing that is,' I exclaimed; 'how I wish we could grow it decently in Britain!'

'Well, yes,' replied Choate, 'it is a pretty plant; but I don't think it can compare with your English may.'

Each of us inclined to prefer the flower with which we are less familiar.

He lived at a time when the huge influx of Far Eastern new plant discoveries was beginning to swell our garden flora, but did not on this account neglect our old garden favourites. His books are well worth reading today and are packed with out-of-the way information.

KENNETH AND DOUGLAS McDOUALL

Logan
THE MULL OF LOGAN · WIGTOWNSHIRE · SCOTLAND
Royal Botanic Garden, Edinburgh

THE FAMILY OF McDOUALL have been living in this area since the thirteenth century. The remnants of an ancient castle remain, but Logan was not noted as a garden for rare plants until James McDouall married a keen gardener, Agnes Buchanan-Hepburn, from East Lothian in 1869. She inspired her two sons, Kenneth and Douglas, so much that through their lives they gardened wholeheartedly, creating one of the most notorious gardens in Scotland. The climate at Logan is very mild, and many of the immense collection of rare and tender plants from all over the world make it a place of pilgrimage to all gardening folk, only surpassed in these islands at Tresco.

The siting on the extreme south-westerly tip of the peninsula is very windy and nothing could be grown without the masses of trees that have given some shelter.

My first contact with Kenneth McDouall was about 1935. The nursery in Surrey where I was employed had acquired the then comparatively new sun roses or helianthemums raised by John Nicoll near Dundee in the earliest decade of the century and named by him after the Scottish mountains. They were thus called the Ben Series, and these it was that the McDoualls wanted and we supplied. We were in touch several times subsequently and invitations given to me to visit Logan. The opportunity did not occur until 1974 when, accompanied by Cuthbert Acland, I made a tour of famous Scottish gardens. The McDoualls had sadly passed on, and, after an interim when the place was owned by Olaf Hambro, the garden had in 1969 been taken into the ownership of the Royal Botanic Garden at Edinburgh. The area actually gardened is about eleven acres, but surrounded by about twelve acres of protective woodland. From being in the doldrums for some years, partly owing to the Second World War, the garden is now an absolute feast of beauty, from rare and tender plants dominated by cabbage palms (*Cordyline*), tree ferns (*Dicksonia*), echiums and various species of *Eucalyptus*. And under them, tucked away everywhere, are plants from warm countries, especially in the southern hemisphere. A visit is an experience not to be missed if you are anywhere near.

In an area of lime-free soil it is obvious that peat-loving plants should take some priority. Before 1926 the McDoualls started a new fashion and expertise in gardening. They used peat blocks to create terraces, a scheme which has been copied in many great gardens since. With adequate rainfall (about forty inches a year) these peat walls and beds of prepared peaty soils are the means by which numerous plants from eastern Asia flourish, such as *Nomocharis*, *Primula*, *Meconopsis*, heaths and *Rhododendron*. Some of the bigger rhododendrons are 150 years old and a great size.

Martin Colledge was Assistant Curator at the time of my first visit and it was fascinating to be introduced to shrubs and plants which I had only known in greenhouses, growing happily in the open air. I can only call attention to a tithe of the tender rarities here: *Olearia*, *Clianthus*, *Crinodendron*, *Carpobrotus*, *Isoplexis*, *Metrosideros*, *Mutisia*, *Chordospartium*, *Myosotidium*, rare magnolias and scented rhododendrons. From spring till autumn there is always something noteworthy to see. Martin gave me a rooted piece of the little creeping fern (*Pyrrosia* sp.) which grows on the fibrous stems of tree ferns. This was established on a tree fern at Trengwainton, Cornwall, while another gift, *Chionochloa conspicua* found a suitable home at Mount Stewart in Northern Ireland – only about thirty miles away across the Irish Sea. It is a lovely white-flowered grass from New Zealand, otherwise known as Hunangamoho grass.

From all the accounts I hear Martin's successor, Barry Unwin, is still doing great things at Logan and the collection of plants, attractively arranged and displayed, continues to flourish. It is not only a unique site but also has been developed with great sensitivity.

THE MESSELS

Nymans
HANDCROSS • SUSSEX
National Trust

Birr Castle
CO. OFFALY • EIRE
The Earl of Rosse

ALTHOUGH IT WAS THE REALIZATION of a dream to be working in Surrey, the home of tree and shrub nurseries on lime-free soils, I was not able to visit any of the great gardens of the Sussex Weald without a car. I managed to purchase a second-hand Austin 7 for £40 in 1936, selling it after the war for £60; which was not bad going. From 1936 until the outbreak of war I made frequent journeys at weekends to such famous places as South Lodge, Wakehurst, Warnham Court and Stonehurst, Leonardslee, Sheffield Park and Nymans. This last enchanted me because it was more of a garden than the arboretums of the others. These and other gardens were fairly frequently opened for charities.

Colonel and Mrs Leonard Messel owned Nymans, which had been started in no small way by the Colonel's father, Ludwig Messel. It was on a hilltop, about five hundred feet up, had superb trees and views and a vast collection of plants, not only placed well in the garden but also grown in nursery rows on the other side of the road. The Colonel was a subscriber to expeditions to western China and elsewhere and the collections of plants were enthralling. He and his wife, Maud, had demolished the grandiose house built by Ludwig and had built a new stone house in the Cotswold tradition. Maud was the great instigator and had a wonderful knowledge of architecture, of furnishing and of historic tastes.

I remember so well my first visit, in early summer, when the Wall Garden was at its best with great shrubs like *Styrax hemsleyanus* and *S. obassia* joined with *Aesculus parviflora* and others to give a sort of higher background to the flowery borders. Elsewhere *Magnolia obovata* was shedding its fragrance around. It was quite obvious that the display had continued from spring onwards judging by the carpets of foliage under the shrubs. But the Colonel had the means and the garden had the conditions for the cultivation of innumerable shrubs and trees such as eucryphias, pittosporums, embothriums, pierises, *Chionanthus* and halesias among others – none of which were grown in the frost-bitten Surrey nurseries. It was a great education in horticulture. I returned with companions again and again and learnt something of the history of *Eucryphia* x *nymansensis* 'Nymansay', rare rhododendrons and such tender treasures as *Asteranthera ovata*, *Berberidopsis corallina* and *Philesia magellanica*, tucked away behind a shady wall. You cross the entrance drive and arrive at the imposing architecture of the shell of the house, much shrouded in climbing plants, to the lawn with its cedars and huge rhododendrons, davidias, eucryphias, magnolias and much besides. Then you have before you a Japanese touch, stone lanterns, a mound with a shelter covered with *Vitis coignetiae* and a long pergola given to various wisterias.

I could go on like this for several paragraphs, but will refer you instead to my book on *Gardens of the National Trust*, for this was one of the first gardens accepted by the Trust for its horticultural merit. In the garden you will find plants raised at Nymans and named after members of the family, including their daughter Anne who became the wife of Michael, the sixth Earl of Rosse, and the renowned James Comber, head gardener for many years, and his successor Cecil Nice.

Michael was already a keen gardener at his home, Birr Castle, Co. Offaly, in Eire. The charming miniature castle was built on a hillock on mainly flat land, but he enriched the surrounds with various shrubs and trees; I did not see it until after his death when Charles Nelson took me, and Michael's son gave us lunch and walked around with us. It was late spring and under every shrub and in every bed around the castle were carpets of *Omphalodes cappadocica*, that wonderful blue relative of the forget-me-not. It was a touch put to the landscape by his mother, Anne. She brought to Birr an eye for good planting. Meanwhile Michael, a dear man, had become chairman of the National Trust's Gardens Panel and we became real friends. In his demesne at Birr he planted scores – even hundreds – of trees of all kinds; as well as numerous conifers, the dated list includes maples, oaks, ashes, limes and many species of the less known genera such as *Nothofagus, Magnolia, Pterocarya* and *Sorbus*. The soil at Birr is on magnesian limestone and he found that this was not inimical to rhododendrons such as the *Triflorum* Series. I have often wondered why there is not another garden where such experiments could be made in the wide territory in north-east Yorkshire where the same formation exists.

But we must return to Nymans because I want to record again how much we owe to Maud Messel in the preservation of old French roses and many species. She was one of a small band of dedicated gardeners throughout the country who had collected and preserved these nineteenth-century roses from old gardens. Edward A. Bunyard, of the then famous nursery at

Eucryphia x *nymansensis*
'Nymansay'

Maidstone, had been helping her before his untimely death and
had indeed produced a delightful book about them. Sadly I
never met him but he was not only a good nurseryman but
erudite about shrubs and plants in general, as his highly
informative articles in *The New Flora and Silva* in the 1930s will
prove. Maud grew her roses partly in a rose garden near the
greenhouses at Nymans, but also in two cottage gardens on the
other side of the road. Here on a beautiful day in late June I
was invited to go and see her collection. I had seen a few in
Ireland and elsewhere but was not prepared for the beauty
spread around, in beds and over hedges and arches in the
perfect setting of a cottage garden. The invitation came after a
fire had made uninhabitable the house at Nymans, and the
colonel asked me to luncheon in their temporary abode ('of
unmitigated ugliness', he said) a few miles away. There we had
the meal, finished with strawberry 'Royal Sovereign' (picked

that morning by James Comber from the Nymans kitchen garden). It was a wonderful awakening to a garden of these treasures, now firmly established once again thanks to the enthusiasm of lovers of beauty in many countries of the north and south hemispheres.

The Messel family did not only suffer from the fire in the house. They also lost much in the way of shelter trees and tall specimens in the great storm of 1986. While it was a disaster to lose choice trees and shrubs throughout the garden, the collapse of several hundred shelter trees, which had initially made the garden such a haven for young specimens, had a notable effect. On my last visit a few years ago I noted and remarked on the greater health of many rhododendrons. Thus do the vagaries of our climate and weather iron out in a big way the little works of man.

W.J. MITCHELL

Westonbirt Arboretum
TETBURY • GLOUCESTERSHIRE
Forestry Commission

EVERYONE WHO GROWS TREES and takes them seriously botanically or for their beauty and longevity must have heard of this great arboretum in Gloucestershire. It was several years before I managed a visit; it had been going for three generations of the Holford family but when I went there it was in the charge of W.J. Mitchell, the Curator. While this book is solely concerned with gardens that were made during the last century it is a publication in which I feel I can pay tribute to Mr Mitchell. He was always very kind to me and took me round the main arboretum in the morning and to Silk Wood in the afternoon. And on one occasion we went across the main road to the magnificent Holford mansion, then and now a girls' school. There was a pond with a magnificent surrounding planting of widely disparate trees and shrubs making a varied tapestry of green. In addition there were some rocks around the water contrasted by the noble foliage of *Hosta sieboldiana*. This was a very early use of this prime plant.

Wherever we went Mr Mitchell would tell me the names of the many trees which were new to me. By the lakeside I expected to see bold clumps of the Westonbirt dogwood, *Cornus alba* 'Sibirica'. But no, Mr Mitchell told me it was such caviare to the rabbits (which abounded in the 1950s) that the few remaining pieces had been transferred to the nursery ground, which was fenced. This struck me as very peculiar and made me wonder whether it was a different *species*, not a form of *C. alba*, which the rabbits ignored. It is a subject which needs looking into by today's botanists.

In the 1950s we were still rationed for certain items, among which was tea. Now, Mr Mitchell was particularly fond of his tea in the afternoon and used to provide it for me, which was refreshing to say the least after an afternoon's walk. But his ration was not enough for him, let alone visitors as well. When I got home and found that the rations for my mother and myself were ample for our needs, a spare packet was sent off to Westonbirt and resulted in a very sincere letter of thanks.

The arboretum was laid out for effect in rigid lines bisected by grass rides with great trees everywhere. Every now and again Mr Mitchell would stray from the rides and show me yet another rarity. Since those days the arboretum has been given a lot of curving, even wriggling, paths and has thereby lost some of its grandeur. In Silk Wood I believe it still remains a wonderful collection of trees and shrubs on both sides of a wide grass walk. By one of the pools were several clumps of the royal fern, *Osmunda regalis*, which build up into astonishing shapes and sizes. In the nursery I was shown a new arrival awaiting transference to a damp site in the arboretum proper; it was *O.r.* 'Gracilis', a charming delicate-looking miniature form. I fell in love with it and on a subsequent visit was given an offset, which, along with a hundred or more other ferns, found their way to Wisley when I moved to a smaller garden. Considering ferns reproduce readily from spores I am surprised it is not more often seen.

But wherever you walk in the arboretum you will, I think, want to return for another look at the Mitchell Drive. This is a wide grass ride, gently curving and as a consequence a wonderful setting for what must have been the most impressive and beautiful of all ornamental plantings in these islands. There were immensely tall conifers as a background on either side tailored down to the hummocks of Japanese maples and all sorts of choice shrubs and small trees in a broken foreground, splendid at all times of the year. No doubt it was Mr Mitchell's favourite walk and was named after him long after the specimens were planted as a compliment to his enthusiastic and able curatorship of some thirty years. The majesty of it remains in my mind.

Westonbirt is not just a place for an hour or two's visit. The guidebook gives us the following revealing figures: it covers 500 acres, there are 17 miles of paths; it is 400 feet above sea level and the tallest tree (a *Wellingtonia*) has achieved 150 feet – just one of a collection amounting to 4000 species and many more varieties.

MARY LOUISE,
DUCHESS OF MONTROSE

Brodick Castle
ISLE OF ARRAN • SCOTLAND
National Trust for Scotland

AFTER OUR VISIT TO STEADSTONE (see page 167), Cubby
Acland and I boarded the ferry to take us to the Isle of Arran.
We landed in the late afternoon and, not being due to visit
Brodick Castle garden until the morning, decided to have a look
at the island. Accordingly we hired a car and made a complete
tour round the coastal road, having superb views of the castle,
the high point of Goat Fell, the wooded or bare landscape and
what our driver said were some of the Duke's shooting lodges
nestling among the trees. It gave us in all a splendid idea of the
whole island and the surrounds of the castle.

The morning was bright and sunny. How we wished that the
the sixth Duchess, Mary Louise, who had restored and enriched
the garden, could have been with us. The climate at Brodick is
very mild, thanks to the North Atlantic Drift (the Gulf
Stream, which meanders off to Iceland instead of embracing
north Britain). Accordingly plants thrive here which would only
be hardy at Logan (see page 171) and in Cornwall and Tresco
on the Isles of Scilly. In fact it is recorded that the Duchess's
son-in-law, Major J.P.T. Boscawen, finding that she was
becoming deeply interested in the garden, arranged for a
steamship full of exotic plants to be sent to Brodick from

Tresco. She had previously received many rhododendrons from Muncaster Castle in Cumbria. With such gifts was her gardening career started; most of these plants, rare species among them, throve at Brodick and I remember many spring shows of the Royal Horticultural Society where the head gardener, John Basford, brought exhibits to remind us of the glories of western Scotland. The Duchess had been brought up at Brodick and therefore knew the climate and some of the possibilities of gardening there.

There is fortunately a stream flowing through the garden and so with the considerable rainfall and shelter from the wooded surroundings not only rhododendrons thrive, but hundreds of primulas, gunnera and many other delightful moisture-loving perennials. It was a fairyland of beauty when we arrived there in June.

But it is not all woodland-loving plants. There are two considerable formal gardens given to summer flowers and terraces below the imposing soft pinky-brown castle. At the time of our visit we were both much impressed with *Echium wildpretii*, which had produced a magnificent spike (over four feet high) of its almost unique brick-red flowers. It was new to both of us. While the formal gardens are mostly lawns with beds of colourful annuals for summer display, on the surrounding walls are many shrubs and climbers, giving their beauty throughout the season. I remember particularly *Actinidia kolomikta*, with every leaf a shade of pink or blush; azaras so covered with flowers that they were of brilliant yet rich yellow, and the scarlet leaves of the Wakehurst *Pieris* as a vivid contrast.

There is no doubt that the Duchess was a keen and successful gardener. She knew how to place plants for their well-being and to make a lovely blend of colour and shape. Here and there, waving in the slightest breeze, were clumps of the New Zealand toe-toe grass, which thrives in Scotland, whereas its close relative, the pampas grass, from South America does not. It opens in summer and lasts through to autumn.

In addition to her prowess as a gardener, the Duchess was also a musician, and, as her daughter the Lady Jean Fforde writes in the excellent guide published by the National Trust for Scotland, she was 'an artist and played the piano and violin beautifully'. How often do music and gardening centre themselves on one individual!

LADY MOORE

Willbrook House
RATHFARNHAM • DUBLIN • EIRE
Garden does not survive

WHETHER ANYBODY TOLD ME to go west when I was a young man, I cannot say, but Ireland, its people and its countryside have always beckoned me. I have been paying visits since the late 1930s, due originally to my friendship with Tom Blythe who was a fellow student with me at the University Botanic Garden, Cambridge. He was a nephew of G.N. Smith of Daisy Hill Nursery, Co. Down. Shortly after the war I spent a fortnight or so in Ireland – only experiencing one wet afternoon – in June; it was then I made my first visit to Willbrook House at Rathfarnham, the home of Sir Frederick and Lady Moore.

Sir Frederick Moore died soon after I met him; he had almost entirely lost his memory ('Some people, Graham, live too long,' Lady Moore had said to me), but his work in horticulture, like that of his father, lives on. Between them they directed the National Botanic Gardens in Dublin for eighty-four years.

I had, I felt, known Lady Moore through being acquainted with *Chaenomeles* – or *Cydonia*, as it was then – 'Phyllis Moore', a rather sprawling plant, admirable on a wall, with fully double flowers of clear bright pink darkening with age to a vivid vermilion pink.

In those days there were no speed restrictions in Dublin. I had hired a car, and on receiving it from the garage was rapidly carried to the outskirts of the city, before daring to turn right or left. I was on my way to Mount Usher, which I must be sure to visit, Lady Moore had told me in a letter (see page 238; I did not regret the instruction, and Mr E.H. Walpole and I became good friends). Eventually I arrived at Willbrook. I have not forgotten the pleasure of my welcome, and the delight at meeting so renowned a gardener and plantswoman. Theirs was a garden of about three acres, with a pleasant curving drive lined with good shrubs and trees. Only the beeches were of great age, because everything else had been planted by the Moores. There were *Nothofagus dombeyi* and *N. antarctica*, *Abies magnifica*, *Picea breweriana* and *P. omorika*, and *Magnolia* x *wieseneri* (syn. *W.* x *watsonii*), that elusive and lovely hybrid whose powerful scent wafts across any garden. When seeds set – as they not infrequently do – the resulting progeny are always *M. obovata* (syn. *M. hypoleuca*) and not *M. sieboldii*, which is thought to be the other parent. Both are specially fragrant. One plant that stays particularly in my memory was what Lady Moore said was the erect form of *Pyrus salicifolia*. The weeping form is well known, but I have never seen the erect form anywhere else. It seemed to be a true *P. salicifolia* – moreover, the Moores were not likely to make a mistake about it – as silvery as the weeper, which rules out related plants like *P. elaeagnifolia, P. nivalis* and others. I wonder whether anyone else remembers this tree, and indeed whether it still lives, or was propagated.

Salix fargesii was there, and the coral-bark maple, *Acer palmatum* 'Sango-kaku'. *Hamamelis mollis* had reached a great size, and *Viburnum grandiflorum* was thirteen feet across.

Willbrook House was stone-built, a good solid building, sitting well in its garden. And everywhere were plants gathered by those two keen spirits, though I felt that, knowing Sir Frederick's predilection for orchids and other greenhouse plants, most had probably been selected by Lady Moore. There was no doubt she not only had an eye for a plant, but knew how to place them in the garden. A great beech tree stood not far from the house, its side and roots fully exposed to the sun, resulting in very dry ground. 'I always choose silvery-leaved plants for that sort of position,' she said, and how right she was. There were *Senecio cineraria* (*Cineraria maritima*), *Artemisia stelleriana*, *Centaurea clementei, Convolvulus cneorum, Phlomis* of several species, and the great silver leaves of *Senecio doronicum*. This produces large orange-yellow flowers and also used to grow well in Ireland, but it would never grow for me in Surrey. Not far from the house was a plant of *Jasminum parkeri* three feet high and four feet across, flowering freely. Along the sunny walls was the gooseberry-leaved rose, *Rosa stellata* var. *mirifica*, from the Sacramento mountains, New Mexico; the flowers are like those of a *Cistus* in magenta pink. The species seems to have died out, but this form is in fairly general cultivation and quite hardy. *Carpenteria californica* was there, too, an especially large-flowered form obtained from Edward Woodall's garden at Nice; I

Rosa stellata var. *mirifica*

suspect the good form grown today as 'Ladhams' Variety' is the same, for Ernest Ladhams had a way of appropriating to himself especially good forms of plants which he found in gardens, such as *Phlox paniculata* 'Elstead Variety', *Actaea matsumurae* (formerly *Cimicifuga simplex*) 'Elstead' and *Erigeron glaucus* 'Elstead Pink', commemorating his interesting nursery, full of good plants. *Dendromecon rigida* had romped up to fifteen feet or so, and the rare *Hippeastrum x acramannii* was at its foot. That apricot-tinted yellow rose 'Climbing Lady Hillingdon', with its contrasting dark coppery foliage, enchanted me. 'She is no good in a bed,' said Lady Moore; 'best against a wall.'

I was at that time collecting the old roses, and it gave me much delight to see the Rugosa rose 'Fimbriata' (sometimes called 'Dianthiflora' or 'Phoebe's Frilled Pink'); it is of pale pink with prettily fringed petals, and a good grower. It thrives at Rowallane, Co. Down. Several other rare old roses were treasured at Willbrook: a huge bush of *R. x hibernica*, found in 1795 near Belfast, believed to be a hybrid between *R. canina* and *R. pimpinellifolia*; *R.* 'Hillieri' (syn. *R. x pruhoniciana* 'Hillieri'), very tall, and *R. farreri*, carefully placed in part shade, which should always be given it if the foliage is to remain green. And then there was the heirloom which Lady Moore has handed down to us and which she named 'Souvenir de St Anne's'. This is a nearly single sport of the original bush 'Souvenir de la Malmaison'; it originated at the Guinness family home, St Anne's near Dublin, which is now a public park with a large new rose garden. I was delighted to find, during my last visit, that a large bed was filled with 'Souvenir de St Anne's'. The bush forms of this rose are constant in production until the autumn, and I rank 'St Anne's' above the original (named by the Grand Duke of Russia in honour of the Empress Josephine's garden, after her death) and its lemon-white sport, 'Kronprinzessin Viktoria'. Lady Moore was a regular exhibitor at the Royal Horticultural Society of Ireland's Rose Group Show, usually taking first prize for a vase of mixed old roses.

The old yellow Scots Briar was just going over; likewise several others of the same family, including the grey-backed purple 'Mary, Queen of Scots'. I remember, too, on one visit being greeted by the sumptuous blooms of tree peonies including *Paeonia* x *lemoinei* 'L'Espérance' and 'Souvenir de Maxime Cornu'.

On another occasion I stayed a couple of nights at Willbrook, a most comfortable home, though a bit old-fashioned. Nellie, the housemaid, and Norah, the cook, looked after the whole of the house for Lady Moore. I was awakened soon after seven a.m. with a large jug of hot water which Nellie brought up to me; she pulled back the curtains and let in the sunlight. On rising, what was my surprise to look down into the garden and see Lady Moore out there picking raspberries for breakfast! She did not waste time, nor was she tolerant of time-wasters. As far as I remember she kept one gardener, and the whole garden was in good order. At the side of the kitchen garden was a broad gravel path and a broad herbaceous border, backed by a wall on which were climbing plants. She did not waste space or opportunities, either! Her love of plants embraced tiny ones like *Veronica prostrata* 'Trehane', whose yellow leaves make so bright a contrast to the vivid blue flowers, *Geranium psilostemon*, bergenias, species of *Eremurus*, and *Aster forrestii* whose orange eyes vie so strongly with the lavender-blue daisies. *Clematis macropetala* was on the wall, and also *Ribes laurifolium*. And in the shade was my first sight of that most beautiful small funkia (as they were then known), *Hosta tokudama* f. *aureonebulosa* 'Variegata' (syn. *H.t.* 'Variegata'), its blue-green leaves striped with yellowish green. This had been a gift from Lady Burnett of Leys, at Crathes Castle (see page 93), where it originated. Lady Moore passed it on to me, and I grew it at Sunningdale Nursery. We worked up a fair stock over the years from division and showed it at Chelsea in our display. By the afternoon of the first day we had to withdraw it from further sales, as we had sold almost our entire saleable stock of seventy spare plants. I often wonder what happened to all the plants, for one seldom hears about it, nor does one see it.

In 1955 Lady Moore took me to Miss Freeman's garden at Cooldrinagh, Laois – a garden well stocked with herbaceous plants, including a light blue *Geranium himalayense* (*G. grandiflorum*) 'Irish Blue' which I have never seen elsewhere. (I was glad to take a plant over with me on my last visit, to re-stock Irish gardens.) There were other lovely visits to Irish gardens, and they prompted me to start collecting the more unusual herbaceous plants, as well as roses. Irish gardens were full of them, to say nothing of Glasnevin.

Lady Moore came to see my garden with Mrs Ruby Fleischmann, an old friend of us both. Ruby asked for a plant of some interest which I had growing – I forget what it was – and Lady Moore said, 'Do you think, Graham, that plant might have a little brother?' This was Lady Moore: keen, kindly, and with a good sense of humour. She had a great influence on Irish horticulture, and I bless her memory.

HEATHER AGNES MUIR

Kiftsgate Court
CHIPPING CAMPDEN • GLOUCESTERSHIRE
Mr and Mrs J. Chambers

IT WAS STRANGE that, early in the century, two such gifted garden-minded people should have started to make what have become famous gardens next door to one another on an escarpment of the Cotswolds above Chipping Campden. They were Heather Muir at Kiftsgate Court and Lawrence Johnston at Hidcote. They were friends and I think they both learnt highly original gardening from each other. Johnston was an architect by profession and may well have had considerable influence on the Muirs' garden, while Heather was very clever at planting and the handling of colours. I had visited Hidcote several times and had noted the imposing gates to Kiftsgate a little way down the hill. On a lovely summer day I paid my first visit and met the owners.

I was quite bowled over by the colour work and the delight of the whole garden. My impression – and great appreciation of it – was recorded in the Royal Horticultural Society's *Journal* for May 1951.

It was not just another Jekyllian colour scheme garden but an intriguing design well handled at the top of the escarpment with lengthy views over the village of Mickleton and beyond. At the bottom of the slope was another garden with magnolias and other trees and shrubs, reached by slopes and steps, with a little pool and fountain halfway down. But that was not all, for the copsy slope up the drive was interplanted with autumn-colouring shrubs and trees. It was an old dwelling and a previous owner had planted lime trees down the long drive and also some maritime pines to break the buffets of wind – which were met by the house – and make the views therefrom the more interesting.

I had never seen colour so well managed before. Apart from some small side borders and beds immediately in front of the garden door we went along two lengthy borders devoted to pinks and purples and grey foliage, cleverly lit by the salmon tone of 'Albertine' rose partnered by the soft mauve-violet of 'William Lobb', a daring combination which, with the isabelline tint of *Lilium x testaceum*, took what might have been a rather dull assembly into the realm of high art.

Extending beyond this pair of borders under a large dark chestnut, the next view was entirely different: one border of yellows and blues and some coppery foliage. In the 1930s a most brilliant pure blue delphinium was 'Mrs Paul Nelke', now lost to cultivation I fear. Here also were grasses and hostas and hypericums, but the background gave the wonderful touch – it was copper beech. Breathtaking, as indeed was the next view of a return border, going back to the house, with two hedges of the striped Gallica rose Rosa Mundi (*R. gallica* 'Versicolor'). Weeping down upon it from above was the largest rose plant in the country, *Rosa filipes* 'Kiftsgate', which is now something like a hundred feet across and ascending a tall copper beech to about forty feet.

And then, past a narrow defile where the soil is lime-free and supports some rhododendrons, we entered the White Garden, with all sorts of white and pale flowers from roses, philadelphus, *Deutzia monbeigii*, hydrangeas and others, brightened by the genuine pure pink *Alstroemeria ligtu*, nowadays much mixed and hybridized with the orange-tinted *A. haemantha*.

In the shady recess of the house was a truly immense plant of *Hydrangea villosa*, though of course not yet in flower. The next treat was tea on the terrace under the pillared portico, with the most succulent gingerbread ever. I have Heather's recipe still!

The garden had been going for perhaps twenty-five years and Heather was always improving it. Apart from her skill with colours she also understood cultivation and that the best results are from well-nurtured soil. Kiftsgate had good soil to start with but it has been fed regularly over the years. She had certainly started gardening by the early 1920s (proved by a bill for some rare and expensive plants), and her enthusiasm for colour in the garden gradually replaced her interest in hunting which had occupied her fairly fully when living near Banbury.

In between the wars Kiftsgate had a staff of five in the garden, and the kitchen garden and greenhouses were well maintained, and as a result the hall and rooms were well decorated with groups of pot plants and flowers. Diany Binny, Heather's eldest daughter, recalls going up to London with flowers for a Royal Horticultural Society competition which captured first prize.

The many staddle stones and their circular caps in the paving down the slopes came from the farm at Hidcote Boyce.

Heather was also the creator of the little pool and summerhouse, halfway down the slope to the lower garden; formerly it was a mere terrace, with *Clianthus puniceus* on the wall at the back. In spite of its siting, Kiftsgate is comparatively warm and hence the success with this plant and also *Chionochloa* (syn. *Cortaderia*) *conspicua* which flaunts its creamy pink plumes at midsummer in the top garden. Apart from an example in a nearby village, and seedlings raised much later at the Chelsea Physic Garden, this is the only example I have seen in British gardens. I wonder why.

Rosa filipes 'Kiftsgate'

Fortunately, Diany Binny and her daughter (and sister)
realize what a brilliant jewel they have to look after and
Kiftsgate Court still takes its place among the great joys of
British gardens. And if you are invited into the house you are
further regaled by murals covering whole walls, paintings of
life-size magnolias and other flowers by Aubrey Waterfield;
thus was the garden brought indoors in 1932.

SIR HAROLD NICOLSON AND VITA SACKVILLE-WEST

Sissinghurst Castle
CRANBROOK • KENT
National Trust

ROSES DREW US TOGETHER – the old French roses of the Gallica breeding. Vita had been drawn to them as well as Constance Spry (see page 225), in whose house we met on a glorious June day. There were the roses, in full flower and scent, growing in stiff clay soil. It was just the same at Sissinghurst, but years of cultivation and mulching have improved the soil immeasurably. The Nicolsons had gone to live in what was an ancient tower and two cottages and devoted their lives to making the buildings habitable and providing a garden around them. Harold was the designer, she was the planter. They had no horticultural training and when I first saw the borders I was not impressed, but after a few years they secured two well-trained gardeners, Pamela Schwerdt and Sibylle Kreutzberger, who by hard work, expertise and devoted attention transformed the whole place and are the cause of the overvisiting today, for their splendid work has been carried on by their successor, Sarah Cook, who spent some years getting to understand the garden under them.

There is no doubt that Harold had design in his blood. Unfortunately, I think the Nicolsons were in a hurry to get the garden into order (it was something of a rubbish heap when

Rosa 'Sissinghurst Castle'

they took over) for in subsequent years when certain hedges had to be reduced it was found that their alignment was faulty, but this might have been deliberate.

The whole estate was given to the National Trust in 1967. And what a gift it was! Mediaeval tower and ancient buildings, part of the original moat and several old walls. Apart from the heavy Wealden clay and the fact that the whole site was open to all the winds from the north-east, it was an ideal spot upon which to turn loose all one's gardening thoughts. Vita's long poem *The Garden* (1946) proved her to be deeply steeped in the beauty of plants and their history.

It is a very wonderful experience to walk down the paved slope under the great tower and to find yourself at once in the garden, with beautiful well-grown plants on every side. Living as they did partly in one cottage, partly in another, with the tower making another, the few steps to their night abode in the open air awakened them to the beauties of white flowers at dusk or even at night. It prompted the making of the white garden – possibly the first in these islands, though the little one at Hidcote and the larger one at Crathes in Scotland may pre-date it. It would be nothing, especially in daylight, without its dark box hedges.

One of the best places to see what an intricate design has been realized is from the top of the tower. The choices of colours for each area are to be seen clearly, not only on a glorious summer's day but also in spring when bulbs give so much beauty, or later when the flowering shrubs have changed to the colours of autumn. Every wall and section has its speciality, blue poppies (*Meconopsis*), velvet of *Clematis* and roses, gentians and *Aster* x *frikartii* and a vast concourse of all the best flowers result in this being one of the most popular gardens with the public. The makers might be embarrassed with it all, but could not be disappointed.

HAROLD AINSWORTH PETO

Iford Manor
WILTSHIRE
Mrs E. Cartwright-Hignett

ONE OF THE GREAT JOYS of the British Isles is that when you travel west you sooner or later find wonderful scenery. This is so very true in Ireland. The sea runs up long estuaries joining hilly, even mountainous country. The wind from the Atlantic is something you have to put up with! But wherever there is shelter from it, there flowers and gardens grow. It is so at Glengariff Bay on the island of Ilnacullin where Annan Bryce with Harold Peto's help and advice started to turn the whole island into a garden.

Helen Dillon very kindly drove Rosemary Brown – both very keen gardeners – Charles Nelson and myself there, one summer's day. I had long wanted to see the garden with its much photographed Italian arch and this was the opportunity. Bryce intended building a dwelling there but the development of the garden seemingly never gave him time to build as he had intended. The space was left, but even though empty it seems in its way to be the heart of the island. There are successful Italian architectural features enough to make the island an inhabited whole, whichever way you turn. And there are some really splendid features to carry you on from one vista to another. Wherever you go you will find species of shrubs and trees of such tenderness as are otherwise only found on Tresco. The climate at Ilnacullin is exceptionally mild. Many trees and shrubs are natives of Australia and New Zealand, South Africa and South America, besides the warmer parts of Europe and Asia. It is a great education not only in botany but also in aesthetics. We spent the whole day there tearing our eyes from shrubs we had never seen before to yet another architectural delight. It started to rain as we left; the little boat was waiting to take us back to the mainland. We all put up umbrellas and got into the boat and caused much amusement to onlookers, but we kept dry!

In his own garden at Iford Manor, Wiltshire, Harold gave full rein to his architectural leanings, adapting an old house picturesquely approached by a noble stone bridge over a river into something very richly Italianate with its paved walks, stone columns, water features and statuary. Another of his great works may be found in the long formal water garden at Buscot Park, Berkshire, which Lord Faringdon left to the National Trust. Here the inventiveness with only a slight slope to provide for variety is astonishing; steps, pools both round and rectangular, bridges and statuary all lead one on to the eventual large lake. When I first went there it was obvious that the many huge elms had been left to accentuate in their height the rather flat land. The elms have sadly gone.

Others of his talented designs may be found at Wayford Manor, Somerset; Heale House, Wiltshire; and West Dean Park and Nymans in Sussex. But wherever you trace Peto's influence you may be sure to find special stone for the buildings and an artist's eye for their placing. He died in 1933.

PHYLLIS REISS

Tintinhull
YEOVIL • SOMERSET
National Trust

WHEN MR AND MRS REISS went to live at Tintinhull they dragged themselves away from their home, Dowdeswell Court near Hidcote, no doubt with some regrets. But they acquired instead a Georgian house of great quality. Of colourful Ham stone, it was so admired by an American that he had it copied exactly and erected in the United States. In due course Phyllis Reiss left her house and garden to the National Trust. Meanwhile she and her husband had worked miracles with the garden.

I think her apprenticeship at her earlier garden had stood her in good stead; she had no doubt tried out her colour schemes and knew what she was about. It was entirely new to me; I had not visited before but was quite bowled over by the handling of the colours. It was not a repeat of all that Jekyll had taught us but something fresh and vibrant. Although not in the Cotswolds it had the same rather heavy, limy soil, so the planting was proscribed.

Colour has been used in different ways in gardens over the centuries. Stark contrast and brightness were much the vogue in Victorian and Edwardian times, but by degrees over the twentieth century softer combinations of colours and grey foliage came into fashion until today, when they are perhaps the dominant note in gardens. Phyllis Reiss struck out on her own.

There had been for many years a garden of sorts, straight down and back, but the Reisses added the best part of an acre to it, at right angles to the main view west. Everywhere were carefully thought-out schemes of plants and colours, which were annually adjusted and polished. One of their largest additions was a central rectangular pool, leading to a summerhouse with stone pillars. The pool was flanked by broad strips of grass behind which were two borders backed by yew hedges. They were filled with most original assortments of colour. One was of scarlet, white and yellow with silvery foliage; height was given by a shower of yellow from the Mount Etna broom and *Eucalyptus gunnii*. The other border, after the excitement of the first, was retiring, composed of flowers of muted tones, pinks and mauves, deep reds and heightened by foliage. Both borders were lightened and united by grassy leaves and the upstanding grey foliage of *Iris pallida* subsp. *pallida*, the only iris of the germanica breed which retains its good foliage until autumn. Another border was given to red roses and shrubs and yellow-leaved *Cornus alba* 'Aurea'. A little garden was given to white flowers. One walked between hedges of roses elsewhere and in Eagle Court (from the stone eagles on pillars which guarded it) was a special planting in a sunny border of *Gladiolus murielae* (*Acidanthera*) and nerines. Whenever your visit took place there was always a border at its best – spring, summer or autumn. I wrote in my *Gardens of the National Trust*: 'If I say that every area has its spring bulbs, every wall its climbers and every plant its bloom in due season, I can stop writing and leave you to explore and learn, as I have done for many years this first-hand garden expertise.'

Not to be beaten by the limy soil, special humus and soil were added to a partially shaded area for azaleas. Phyllis told me she had much advice and help from John Scott, famous nurseryman at nearby Merriott. What she did not explain to me was the strange fact that her choice of colours in the house did not appear to be governed by the same thoughts as were her flowers outside. Indoors I found the colours hard and thick.

Seeing the success she had in the garden, she was asked whether she would help the Trust by keeping her eyes on the flower borders at nearby Montacute House. Vita Sackville-West had been doing so for some years but found the journey from Kent arduous and wished to give up. Her borders had been filled with soft colours though the great mansion was dominating in its yellowish Ham stone. Phyllis took the job under her wing but gradually removed many of the soft colours and grey foliage and gave the borders strong and vibrant tints which I thought was wise. The whole garden was run by two very able gardeners and we instituted a number of changes and improvements such as the realignment of the verges of the vast lawns which had been eaten away over the years by injudicious paring and straightening. A whole foot was added to one lawn by bringing the edge forward and infilling with soil.

THE RENTONS

Branklyn
PERTH · SCOTLAND
National Trust for Scotland

ON MY ARRIVAL IN SURREY in the early 1930s I lost no time in cycling to Wisley, the Royal Horticultural Society's garden near Woking. There I met the curator of the rock garden, John Wall.

Our friendship lasted for many years. On more than one occasion I met there a close friend of his, Geordie Duncan, who had a small garden at Isleworth, on heavy clay soil, where he grew an astonishing number of choice plants. Whenever he could he went up to Scotland and always came back with a new plant or two for his garden, mostly from Branklyn. It seemed that there was a remarkable collection of plants, on a par almost with the Royal Botanical Garden at Edinburgh. But it was not until after the war that I was able to travel so far. A visit to Branklyn was eagerly anticipated and did not disappoint. I was thrilled with all I saw. Just under two acres, the whole garden was packed with plants, collected with a sure eye by Dorothy Renton. Moreover I think I can add that my visits made me realize what true kindness and friendship – to say nothing of plantsmanship – were when given by John and Dorothy. I do not remember ever coming away from a garden with such delight, stored in my whole being.

They had started the garden in 1922 and throughout their lives devoted themselves to its well-being and gradual enlargement, to keep pace with their desire for more and yet more plants. I do not know whence they gained their expertise in gardening; probably some was inherited and much more was acquired by garden visiting through the years. It was always in impeccable order, as one wandered through the narrow paths from one choice plant to another. For so small a garden it was remarkable how they found space for quite large-growing trees. There were many of them, with dozens of good shrubs and special rhododendrons of all sizes, down to perennials and alpines and bulbs. Everything was placed to provide the utmost beauty from it, associated with its neighbours. I have only come across one other garden which approached it for charm, delight and satisfaction, and that was A.T. Johnson's in North Wales (see page 142).

Shrubs and trees, as they grew to maturity, altered the banks and levels from warm sunny places to cool and shady positions. Thus the owners had to be continually on the lookout to see whether new sites required replanting or the underplanting needed resiting. Apart from work on the initial placing of rocks for three rock gardens and a large scree, they had only one helper through the years. The rocks for the first and second slope were lime free; those for the third, limy. Here was a practical division which served them well.

It was not a garden sunk in the beauty of natural scenery, but might even be called a town garden from its proximity to Perth, and so Dorothy could indulge herself with plants of any and every kind. From the alpine house to the retaining walls, the steps and pool to the wider slopes, everything was done to make the garden beautiful and full of colour throughout the year. Early bulbs and alpines, lovely woodland plants and shrubs of all possible categories, reaching up to the trees – the golden Atlantic cedar, cherries, maples and the like, with plenty of specimens and shrubs with summer leaf colour – variegated, golden or what we misleadingly call 'copper'. And then the autumn tints started, carrying on till the colour comes mainly from bark and berries, and the winter flowering shrubs. There was never a dull moment. In the fullness of time they left their house and garden to the National Trust for Scotland who maintain and develop it well. How lucky I was to have met Geordie Duncan who first encouraged me to visit the Rentons – and other Scottish gardens!

In a short appreciation like this I cannot call attention to more than an appetizer of the plants they grew so well. But a little list would start with *Meconopsis* (George Sherriff Group) 'Branklyn', a magnificent dark blue hybrid, and *Paeonia* 'Branklyn'. No doubt there are other plants which we owe to

Erythronium dens-canis
and (above)
E. 'Pagoda'

them. They grew species of *Nomocharis*, many primulas, gentians, azaleas and rhododendrons, *Ranunculus lyallii* and notholirions, trilliums, erythroniums, lilies and that little charmer *Paraquilegia anemonoides*. *Stellaria chamaejasme* is also there, with many conifers and ferns to add solidity to the view. In company with the Botanic Garden at Edinburgh, they embarked on a series of peat walls, where grew many small ericaceous plants; I believe these walls were among the first of their kind in the country. The plants included a great collection of the genera *Gaultheria*, *Vaccinium*, *Shortia*, *Cassiope* and the like. The visitor comes away almost bemused by the wide variety of plants; two veterans are so imposing that they make subsequent visiting a pilgrimage to Dorothy's and John's enterprise and enthusiasm − and skill. They are the old specimen, some ten feet high, of *Acer shirasawanum* 'Aureum' and the great *Betula albosinensis* var. *septentrionalis*. I bless Geordie Duncan again.

WILLIAM ROBINSON

Gravetye Manor
EAST GRINSTEAD • SUSSEX
Gravetye Manor Hotel

DESPITE THE FACT THAT I did not have the good fortune to meet him; that he has a really lovely biography, *William Robinson 1838-1935 Father of the English Flower Garden* by Mea Allen (1982); that his *The English Flower Garden* of 1883 has had so many editions and been in print for so long, I feel that this little book would be incomplete without a few paragraphs about William Robinson – though perhaps his most productive years were before 1900. On the other hand his creation of garden and estate at Gravetye was from 1885 onwards. To put it briefly he purchased the old stone manor house, laid out the garden and gradually added farms and other small properties until he had accumulated over a thousand acres of lovely countryside, which he proceeded to beautify further by planting trees.

Subsequently the manor house, after years of neglect following his death, was purchased by Peter Herbert and has been turned into one of the country's most noted hotels. And gradually Peter has restored Robinson's famous garden. The last big venture was the restoration and restocking of the almost circular kitchen garden. The estate is run by the Forestry Commission.

Prior to his coming to the manor house, William Robinson had no garden of his own of any size. For years he had preached the gospel of the beauty of natural growth and informal gardening, but it must have surprised many people to find that around the house the garden was on formal lines – as indeed it should be. In practically all great gardens the formality of the rooms in the house is met again on entering the garden. After that introduction to natural beauty we have Robinson to thank for the informality of many great gardens today.

Robinson continued to practise what he preached. Here is an extract from his preface to *Gravetye Manor*, written in 1911:

> One day, Mr Mark Fisher, the landscape painter, was sketching the flower garden, and [a] yew hedge formed the extreme end of the picture. He said to me 'Why don't you give me a free hand there instead of a hard black one?' The remark struck me very much. Next autumn I took

away the hedge of Yews. [He planted roses and clematis instead.] The lesson I never forgot; we abolished the shears and clipped no more.

It was not only the design of gardens that received such basic criticism; he was an ardent plantsman, and many of the entries in *The English Flower Garden*, edition after edition, contained concise paragraphs on plants new to our gardens and notes on their cultivation. He lived till 1935 and at a very advanced age went to Gertrude Jekyll's funeral. This is the more remarkable because for many years he could only move about in a wheeled chair or car, owing to, initially, an accident to his spine when jumping over a stile on the way back from church in the company of E.A. Bowles. The records prove him to have been a strong and athletic man. He was tended by a devoted nurse to the end of his days.

I have been to his splendid garden many times in recent years and it has been faithfully restored and tended. There are many noble shrubs and trees in about thirty acres though the great storm of 1986 ravaged it. Some two hundred trees fell. I particularly remember a great specimen of *Rhododendron* 'Christmas Cheer' in full flower in March; it only flowers at Christmas in the warmer west! And there are three or four tall specimens of *Magnolia virginiana* (*M. glauca*) about ten feet high which bear quantities of deliciously scented cream flowers in summer, after all frost has gone. It is truly a great garden and proves Robinson's wide-ranging love of plants, specially naturalized bulbs of many kinds.

Fortunately in 1984 Peter Herbert managed to persuade Sagapress of New York to republish his great book *Gravetye Manor or Twenty Years' Work round an old Manor House*. Peter honoured me very much by asking me to write an Introduction

Rhododendron 'Cilpinense', Rh. 'Ptarmigan' and Rh. 'Praecox'

for it. One of Robinson's paragraphs from this book should be quoted here as a final *envoi*:

> The aim was, as it always should be, to get as near the visible beauty of things, as it is possible for the artist to go. Clear and loving eyes see enough of the divine beauty of sky, sea, field and tree, ever to wish for more than getting as near a faithful record as the winged minutes and ceaseless changes in sky and land allow to human effort.

JAMES P.C. RUSSELL

Sunningdale Nursery
WINDLESHAM • SURREY

THROUGH THE EARLY PART of the twentieth century Harry White ran Sunningdale Nursery. His special love was for rhododendrons – of all kinds, species and hybrids. My meeting with him is recorded in my book *Three Gardens*. He died just before the Second World War. Louis Gray, his office man, was therefore in charge and I met him several times there. He had acquired a good knowledge of everything. But the nursery was put on the market and was bought by Norman Hamilton Smith with a view to its being just what Jim Russell needed, Jim being the son of a distant cousin of his. Jim had been invalided out of the army early in the war.

Jim loved plants and used to grow alpines in pots on his windowsill at Eton. He and his parents and sister moved into the rather crazily built rooms in the nursery house, and Jim, having a remarkably able and astute brain, speedily absorbed all that Louis Gray could teach him, especially the propagation of rhododendrons by layering and also by cuttings in glass bell-jars. Between them and with much hard work and additional labour the nursery was restored to something like order, with new greenhouses and sheds, while retaining all the big old specimens of trees and shrubs which Harry White had nursed. It was the specimens and Jim's love of beauty which led him to turn the place into a sort of show ground. The soil was very varied, from heavy clay to light sand and deep black bog. He laid out a formal garden by the house, a bog garden and two very long, broad borders for shrubs and plants. In addition he employed a Frenchman, a M. Goor, to make two pools, and a wall and plinth at the end of the borders to accommodate his superb statue of Pallas Athene, which eventually I believe found its way into the British Museum.

It was quite obvious that Jim was a man of great ability and ideas, and he had acquired a sound knowledge of plants and their needs, though he had no real training in horticulture. The direct result of all this was that he was called in to advise on the planting and layout of many great gardens throughout the British Isles. In due course he asked me to come and run the nursery for him. It so happened that I was ready for a move from the managership of the wholesale nursery of T. Hilling and Co. of Chobham, near by, and I accepted the offer and spent the next fifteen years or so busily there. My employment was only part-time because I had recently accepted the post of Gardens Adviser to the National Trust – also part-time.

After about twelve years of, for me, a close and enjoyable partnership at Sunningdale, Jim moved on to Castle Howard, Yorkshire, and settled himself in The Dairies, a charming classical stone-built dwelling on the estate. He took with him some of his own favourite plants including some large rhododendrons. George Howard, an old friend of Jim's, wanted help in developing the grounds to make them more attractive to the public. As a consequence Jim laid out a large rose garden, mostly with old French varieties with which he had become enthused, but also with attractive shrub roses and some other plants to prolong the display. A very famous part of the grounds, Ray Wood, was given a new look with many superb shrubs, all well distributed. But Jim's mind was large and before long he started what was his major contribution to British horticulture, a huge and detailed arboretum at Castle Howard covering many acres of varied land, moist and dry with some mixed woodland included, a stream and a lake. The list he compiled with the help of Michael Lear must be the most exhaustive ever undertaken in these islands and the planting and labelling was done, mostly unaided, by Jim himself, using quite little plants. It was of such importance that the Royal Botanic Gardens, Kew, have taken it under their wing. There is an immense list extant with the position of planting, the height, the origin, donor and so on. He raised the plants from seeds collected in the wild and from cuttings in his greenhouses, and until the sudden great increase in world prices of oil, grew many tropical plants.

Jim went on two major expeditions collecting plants and seeds, in western China and Mexico. He raised and named several rhododendrons such as 'Coromandel' and 'Thunderstorm'.

Finding that the younger Howards were not really interested in gardening and all it represented, Jim left Castle Howard after George's death and went north, ending his days in eastern Scotland, much mourned by all who knew him. He never took what is called 'a holiday' but went on helping people with their gardens to the very end. I do not think it is an exaggeration to say that he was one of the most noted and able gardeners of the late twentieth century and had a far-seeing brain. Like many great gardeners before him, he started life with alpines and ended with trees which he could not hope to see in maturity. Such is the faith of an all-embracing plantsman.

MOLLY AND NOEL SANDERSON

Ishlan

BALLYMONEY · CO. ANTRIM · NORTHERN IRELAND

BOTH MOLLY AND NOEL were medical doctors, but for rather over thirty years managed to run an acre or two of garden which became well known for the wonderful collection of plants it contained. Molly was a great seeker after rare and beautiful plants, concentrating in early years on alpines, but as time went on she embraced perennials and even shrubs. She would not have wished it to be called a great garden but rather one where she grew all her treasures so well.

This is how I found it on my one and only visit, kindly arranged by Charles Nelson who was my guide to little-known gardens in Ireland. We were given a warm welcome as a prelude to a most pleasurable and instructive visit. There was no place for weeds: cultivated specialities were everywhere, many acquired from far-away gardens. I remember particularly (because they were in flower at the time) the extra wide-collared *Eryngium* x *zabelii* which was named by Leslie Slinger 'Donard Variety' after his famous nursery, and a superb white-flowered form of *Dicentra eximia*, *Thalictrum lucidum* and of course the little black viola named 'Molly Sanderson'. This is as black as the little plant well known before the war as 'Black Knight' but which I think has become extinct.

Other plants which originated at Ishlan are the handsomely variegated *Eryngium planum* 'Molly Sanderson', which is in the care of Gary Dunlop in Co. Down, and *Hosta tokudama* 'Molly Sanderson', which has leaves wholly pale greenish yellow.

Molly believed fully that in order to preserve a plant you should give it away to keen people. I hope her ideals will eventually bear fruit with all the plants she knew and loved so well. This is really the crux of the matter. Molly and Noel took to gardening in middle age and grew up, so to speak, with their garden. The soil was heavy, fairly neutral and much of it sloped towards the sunshine. They worked very hard, making a formal pool and paved terraces which gave a firm setting to the house. Alpine plants were one of their first delights but their enthusiasm had no bounds, only recurring fevers! They planted trees and shrubs and generally furnished the whole place so that there was always something to see, coming into flower or berry, or autumn colours.

They were wise in three ways. Studying the soil and its possibilities; leaving a sloping lawn empty to help to balance the densely planted beds and borders and rock garden; and having the wit to retire from it before the upkeep got beyond them. This is something we should all bear in mind rather than having to watch a loved garden overwhelming our capabilities.

SIR ERIC SAVILL, THOMAS HOPE FINDLAY AND JOHN BOND

The Savill Garden
WINDSOR GREAT PARK • BERKSHIRE
Crown Estate

WITH THE PASSING of three distinguished Keepers of the Savill Garden, I think it best in this instance to give the above title to this entry, confirming as it does the name of the originator. Since it was mooted in 1932 it has become one of the most famous gardens in the British Isles.

It so happened that I came to Surrey in 1931, from cold and limy Cambridge, and within a very few years had heard of this great endeavour of Mr Eric Savill's all-embracing mind, which had the blessing of George V and Queen Mary. The Queen was deeply interested in gardens and plants. She never missed a Chelsea Show and I remember how in many years the press photographer would capture her being handed over the little bridge which Robert W. Wallace seemed to have ready for her in his big garden outside the marquee.

The love of gardens and flowers continued well into the reigns of Edward VIII, who was a very keen gardener, and into that of George VI and Queen Elizabeth, later to be the Queen Mother. She came of a gardening family: her brother, the Honourable David Bowes-Lyon, inherited a fine historic garden in Hertfordshire and became President of the Royal Horticultural Society. Later the gardening enthusiasm has again awakened in the Prince of Wales. So it seems very right and proper that Windsor Great Park should have a fine garden and this is what has transpired, with the original site chosen by Eric Savill having all the advantages in soil and setting that could be desired, coupled with a stream and ponds.

In the 1930s Eric Savill came to the large wholesale nursery where I was to become manager and we spent a whole morning together choosing trees for his brainchild. Later, at Sunningdale Nursery, he asked for a quantity of *Nothofagus obliqua* which had seeded themselves under a big old tree. These are now in a row along the drive from Cumberland Gate, leading past the wonderful collection of *Rhododendron* species which came as a gift from J.B. Stevenson's great garden, Tower Court, near Ascot. Moving full-sized specimens into new quarters was a mammoth task. Above this exhaustive assembly of rhododendrons is the heather garden and the dwarf conifer collection. They are on a site where gravel had been quarried, and thus of varied levels and outline, besides which the dry gravelly soil is just what is required as a spartan diet for the dwarf conifers.

Rhododendron moupinense

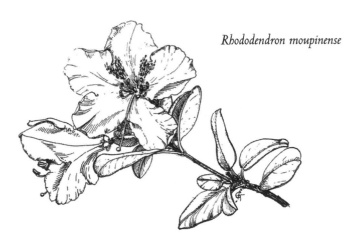

Eric was knighted for his gardening enterprise by George VI. Although he was not a trained gardener but a chartered surveyor, he brought his able brain to benefit the park in many ways. In 1947 he was joined by Thomas Hope Findlay, as assistant. Hope came of a noted gardening family: his father had been in charge of the Royal Horticultural Society's garden at Wisley and his brothers had also been eminent in horticulture. He later became Keeper of the Savill Garden in succession to Eric. In the meantime the garden continued to grow, allied to the Valley Garden where a great assembly of trees and shrubs is found. Throughout its development rhododendrons and azaleas predominated but magnolias of all kinds are very evident.

But in due course his place was taken by John Bond who brought immense knowledge coupled with sincere drive, and the collections of ferns, plants and bulbs, shrubs and trees grew at a great pace. John had spent some years at Hillier and Sons' famous nursery in Hampshire and so was conversant not only with the growing but also the propagation of all woody plants. He simply could not stop and so today the Savill Garden has an almost unrivalled collection of plants of all kinds. Some of his most noted contributions to the vast assembly are dwarf conifers and hollies. There was limitless space, easily worked sandy soil, ample means and a dedicated staff. To all this was added a varied terrain and age-old leafmould. I remember John Bond telling me that in using the park's accumulated leafmould they only went once in ten years to the same area for supplies!

But wherever you go during the year you may be sure of finding some spectacular display. There are millions of dwarf bulbs naturalized for February and March through to the flaming splendour of May and June, and autumn-flowering crocuses and cyclamens for late months. There is one special boggy woodland spot where hardy orchids, various blue poppies (*Meconopsis* species and hybrids) and literally yards of trilliums grow, with erythroniums seeding about everywhere. The big weeping willow (planted where the garden was started) still graces the pond. And recently the Temperate House has been rebuilt and is a joy to enter when spring is just not warm enough. We owe a lot to three great brains. All of them have been honoured with the greatest horticultural awards. These few paragraphs hardly do justice to what is acknowledged to be a wonderful achievement.

DAVID SHACKLETON

Beech Park
CLONSILLA • CO. DUBLIN • EIRE
Privately owned

DAVID SHACKLETON HAD BEEN DEEPLY INTERESTED in gardening and garden flowers for many years, but I did not have the good fortune to meet him until late in our lives. I had heard much about the wonderful things he grew and was therefore all agog when an invitation came to Rosemary Brown of Graigueconna, Bray, Co. Wicklow, with whom I was staying, to bring me over to Beech Park to lunch. He had an old family bungalow which stood on rising ground surrounded by beech and other trees and approached by a lengthy drive. We had a great welcome from David and his wife. In the main room was an immense plant of *Woodwardia radicans*, a somewhat tender fern of great beauty.

Meconopsis x *sheldonii* 'Slieve Donard'

There was little garden around the house but after lunch we crossed the old yard and entered the walled garden of about three acres. It had at one time no doubt been the kitchen garden and had sundry straight paths; one around the whole area and others crossing and dividing the central part. I think David had added others to take full advantage of shady and sunny sites.

It was summertime and the beds and borders were full of flowers shedding fragrance around. I went again in subsequent years in different months and so my memories of the plants in flower are confused. But there seemed to be everything there: an enormous variety of herbaceous plants, special bulbous plants, alpine plants on raised beds, a few small shrubs, climbers on the walls and two small unheated greenhouses.

Several glorious groups of blue poppies were at their best, making me regret the dry air of Surrey where I live; *Cypripedium*, *Astelia*, *Begonia grandis*, *Jovellana*, *Phyllodoce*, *Phlox*, *Crocosmia*, and more species of *Celmisia* than I had ever dreamed of appeared to be completely at home in the cool nearly frost-free garden. There were white aconitums, *Watsonia beatricis*, daphnes, and on a sunny wall a mass of *Lonicera x americana*, the splendid rich pink, non-twining honeysuckle – in fact almost anything one could imagine. This was not altogether surprising because David, sometimes accompanied by Helen Dillon, the gifted gardener from Dublin, would every year or so make foraging expeditions to different nurseries in the British Isles and would return after about a week with a car heavily laden. But neither these expeditions nor his ability to raise tiny seedlings to flowering stage could have accounted for his success in growing plants of all kinds had he not been a born gardener. A visit to his garden resulted in one coming away humbled.

TIM SMIT

Heligan Gardens

MEVAGISSEY • ST AUSTELL • CORNWALL

FEW OF US CAN REALIZE what life was like in the large estates
before the Great War. From earlier beginnings the Tremayne
family purchased about a thousand acres in the mid-sixteenth
century in the lovely valley leading down to the fishing village
at Mevagissey. So great was the holding that if anything went
wrong with buildings, sheds, walls, fences or trees one did not
have to call in a firm for repairs but obtained the services of a
tenant, for all walks of life were covered. The Great War upset
all this and things have never been quite the same again. The
early history of Heligan is covered in the first pages of the
admirable guide to the Lost Garden by Tim Smit, a Dutchman
who, it is no exaggeration to say, was captivated by what was
left after seventy years of complete neglect. The house had
meanwhile passed into other hands.

Tim Smit decided that there was a project here well worthy
of close attention and years of arduous work. But by
harnessing the help of many experts, archivists, nature lovers
and diverse bodies he has in some twelve years restored an
astonishing array of historic buildings, roads and paths,
streams and ponds, and given new life to the few trees and
great shrubs that still existed. It seems that most of the
ancient garden was overrun by a high covering of brambles,
fallen trees, decaying vegetation and silt. The guide takes you

step by step through these years of clearance, revealing exciting relics of the past.

To my regret it all started when I had become too old to travel and see it, but I had seen another property in a like state and can visualize something of what confronted Tim and his associates. After much restoration it is now already extremely interesting to the visiting public. Once again there are traditional greenhouses and frames for the growing of pineapples and melons with heat provided by decomposing dung (as it was before the use of the fossil fuels of today), vegetable and flower plots and many replanted trees and shrubs, including a replaced avenue of *Cornus capitata*. This thrives in the warm climate of Cornwall, casting a shimmer of silvery yellow over the garden landscape in summer. There are magnificent rhododendrons, introduced by the early plant and seed collectors of the nineteenth century, once again standing proudly over their neighbours.

Clearly shown on a plan of 1770 is the Northern Summerhouse, an elegant, arched building which, like all other buildings in the garden, has been restored using as far as possible the same materials as were originally used. There is an old mount dating from the early seventeenth century, a crystal grotto, an Italian garden, a large greenhouse and of course the head gardener's office whence he controlled the twenty-two outside staff and their twenty counterparts under glass. It must be remembered that in the old days a great country estate like this looked upon the workers as part and parcel of the whole and they were housed by the establishment.

There is still much to be done, I believe, including an assault on further brambles in the valley and innumerable sycamore seedlings. The ditches, gulleys and streams need clearing; the name 'Heligan' means 'The Willows' in Cornish, indicating that there was a considerable rainfall.

When you read that there were houses for bananas, peaches and citrus, a vinery and a big ornamental greenhouse besides acres of flowers and vegetables and woodland walks leading around the slopes where lovely trees, shrubs and plants were growing, the staff does not seem excessive for an age before mechanical contrivances became commonplace.

Taken all in all the restoration was a mammoth task and has been nobly tackled. Long may it survive. It is well worth exploring and all I have known who have paid a visit have come away enthralled by the picture of the past brought to life. The restoration has revealed how many of the old crafts survive among workers today.

DR B.T.D. SMITH

Sidney Sussex College
CAMBRIDGE

IN MY SECOND YEAR at the Botanic Garden at Cambridge, I was in the potting shed when Mr Preston, the Superintendent, came in with three visitors. They were Mr and Mrs Gordon from Whittlesford and Dr Smith, the Dean of Sidney Sussex College. They brought some choice plants which were placed in my hands and I was introduced to them. All three were very keen gardeners and by great good luck I was invited to visit their gardens – my first introduction to gardens at large. Whittlesford was within cycling distance and the Gordons being very friendly and kind welcomed me and we became friends over the immediate years.

Hearing that I was deeply interested in alpine plants, the Dean invited me to see his rock garden at the college on Saturday afternoon. It was a wonderful happening and our friendship lasted until his death some forty years later. Though always very kind and friendly, he was a quiet man and loved gardening. He did not marry, but later became a tutor at the college. The garden of the college covered two or three acres, which were divided between him and the Master – who was not really interested in gardening. They both employed a man to do the mowing and various chores.

My visit was soon after Dr Smith had built with his own hands a sizeable rock garden of Derbyshire limestone using rather small brick-like pieces. He had throughout his life a formal approach to gardening and liked straight lines. Sited as it was against a high brick wall and finished by another wall, he designed a straight path leading down from a curved garden seat, with a few steps – with rocks mainly to one side – to a formal pool and fountain. There was a good scree bed filled with Kabschia saxifrages, campanulas and other treasures, and all the banks of rocks held a liberal assembly of the best alpines, with shady positions for ramondas and haberleas. Some water plants graced the pool – *Butomus umbellatus*, calthas and *Pontederia*. Over the pool a great broom – *Cytisus* 'Dorothy Walpole' – spread her arching branches, bearing myriads of rich crimson and pink flowers. It was a beauty, though now somewhat overlooked because of a plant of similar colouring but larger flowers: 'Burkwoodii'. I little thought that, though I never met Dorothy, the Walpoles of Mount Usher, Co. Wicklow, would become friends of mine in later years.

On the walls Dr Smith grew *Clematis alpina* and *C. macropetala* and many other plants; he also had a good selection of dwarf conifers dotted around. But that was not all. A long straight border was given to a wide variety of herbaceous plants. Though the gravelly, old town soil might grow good alpines, it needed a lot of feeding to grow border plants, and he had installed an automatic system of watering – tall detachable pipes each with a rose at the top, the whole managed by one tap. The setting, with a few big old trees and seemingly endless lawns, was an eye-opener. Later in the summer I went again and found *Lilium davidii* in great clumps down the border. They were easy to grow in that soil and two or three bulbs were given to me for my little garden. Bearded irises were another favourite of Dr Smith's and I gloated over them. It was just at the time when the French and American breeders were producing the 'smoky' toned hybrids such as 'Alcazar', 'Lent A. Williamson' and 'Dominion'. These have all been surpassed by clearer colours, except the highly prolific 'Alcazar' which is still to be seen in many gardens.

Gradually our friendship grew and I was encouraged to go about tea-time on Saturdays; there was always tea and chocolate biscuits in his big room in the new building. In later years he completed his rock garden by adding rocks to fill the rest of the rectangle, this time with large pieces of weathered Westmorland limestone. On losing his gardener he engaged the services of James Blades, who had been the kind and able foreman at the Botanic Garden, and who had taught me so much.

When Dr Smith retired he went to live at Milton Lilbourne in Wiltshire. He started gardening again in a big way on lime-free soil. Thus was he able to grow rhododendrons and other lime-haters to perfection. His garden was about an acre, and well stocked with flowering trees, shrubs, shrub roses, herbaceous plants, in fact everything from early bulbs to the phloxes, after which the garden seemed to pall in his way of thinking. I used to drop in on my journeys to and from the gardens of the National Trust and was always welcomed. He had moved to Wiltshire to be near the River Test; next to gardening his great love was for fishing and he leased a length of the river for several years. We made some trips together to famous gardens, including Hidcote. He enriched my life with much kindness, plants and books – and of course there were always chocolate biscuits with the tea!

CONSTANCE SPRY

Winkfield House
WINDSOR • BERKSHIRE
Privately owned

THERE IS NO DOUBT that Constance Spry made us all look at plants with a different eye. Before she got busy with new ideas, flower arrangers had already come a long way, but in great houses with great gardens the pursuit had been left in the hands of the great head gardeners, much more than the owners of the establishments who might have been more artistic. As it was, flower arranging for big parties in large rooms developed a tradition which owed much to the formal handling of prize flowers, often produced at considerable cost in greenhouses. Constance changed all this.

Apart from being an enthusiastic grower of plants she showed us that every growing thing, not just flowers, had beauty and could be brought into use in the house. I think she was the first to value lichen-covered twigs and branches and she gave as much thought to the use of foliage as to flowers.

I had met her more than once in the 1930s but we really came together near the end of the Second World War. She wrote me from Kent saying that she was going to move house and could I possibly propagate for her new garden her old French roses, mostly the products of the nineteenth century? It was not an easy request; the large nursery where I was manager was mostly given over to the production of farm crops and vegetables. I thought I had better go and see what it all involved. And there in a room mainly white with some gilt frames containing mirrors or pictures, was a large oval table covered with a pale green cloth and a central bowl of the most wonderful arrangement of purplish and murrey-coloured roses of the previous centuries. I had seen a few on a visit to Daisy Hill Nursery, Newry, Co. Down in Northern Ireland before the war but had not been impressed with them. Their shapes and colours were foreign to my eyes – white, pink, crimson, mauve and darkest murrey (often wrongly called maroon, which indicates brown). I had been brought up on shapely Hybrid Teas from which the bluish tints had been deliberately expunged in preference to the sharper yellows, salmons and flames, which came into vogue gradually from 1800 onwards.

As a nursery we were allowed to retain a nucleus of ornamental stock for use after hostilities had ceased. But I was completely bowled over by the soft old colours so beloved in the eighteenth and nineteenth centuries. We did our little bit to grow four or five of each for Constance's new garden, which surrounded a large house which she was going to use for a girls' finishing school near Windsor in Berkshire. Property, especially large houses, was cheap in those days. I expect the accommodation afforded the necessary amount of rooms and space but the garden, of some

CLOCKWISE FROM TOP LEFT: *Rosa* 'Violette', *R.* 'Veilchenblau',
R. 'Goldfinch', *R.* 'Bleu Magenta' *and R.* 'Rose-Marie Viaud'

three acres, was not an asset, being on heavy clay with a large canal or formal pond all open to the east wind.

Constance had been at the forefront of the widening appreciation of the old roses and had acquired before the war all the varieties she could find; a few in this country, but mainly from a nursery in France (Pajotin-Chédane) and of all places Bobbink and Atkins in New Jersey in the United States. Both of these firms went out of business during the war. But roses were only a part of the story.

Constance had a wonderful way of engendering enthusiasm and loyalty from her staff. They were all dedicated to the many fresh ideas that she brought forth. A glance through her several books amply proves this. We became great friends and after the war it was a lovely treat to me to hear the familiar voice saying, 'Are you busy this evening? If not what about coming over for supper?' Some delectable food was always laid before us in a charming dining room where she and her husband 'Shav' Spry and several of the principal staff foregathered after the day's work. The name 'Shav' originated from his being looked upon as a smart young 'shaver' in earlier days. With all this kindness and interest around me, what could I do but bring to her notice rare and new plants?

After the evening meal was over she was not idle. Her needle was always busy. Captivated by the pictures in the renowned *Temple of Flora* by J.C. Thornton of 1812, she started making designs to immortalize yet again the beauty of flowers, in wool. They were done one at a time in large squares: auriculas, tulips, melons and others, all with a plain pale greeny-grey background. They were then reproduced by a carpet manufacturer and the results were different-sized mats and a carpet (which she had in her drawing room). I have two of the mats and they are wearing well and give me much pleasure.

The school thrived and new classrooms were built. More staff were added and I got to know Val Pirie, her partner and also a keen cultivator of plants, and Rosemary Hume, also her partner but in a London cookery school. Enthusiasm was always vibrant. She went to great trouble to improve the soil by adding sharp sand and/or peat for some plants and also by the traditional slow baking of turves by using them to cover a large bonfire of logs. The baking made the soil friable but was a big undertaking. A greenhouse of some size adjoined the house and here all manner of choice things grew, including tender roses, 'Maréchal Niel' and 'Niphetos', tender scented rhododendrons, mimosa and lots of bulbs from the Cape and elsewhere.

A long wall facing east finished the strip of garden between road and canal, with much more beyond. Here quantities of sharp sand were added in an effort to grow pinks and there was of course a long hedge of philadelphus of several kinds. These were much pruned (by cutting for indoors) and the result was long wands of scented flowers. These drop their petals rather quickly when cut, but by immediately removing all leaves they lasted for several days and were in demand for weddings and parties. Constance gave a tremendous boost to the appreciation of flowers and leaves of all kinds and well did she know how to use them, sometimes mixed together, or maybe used singly; lichened branches, eucalyptus foliage and of course the old roses. She was always so cooperative and kind with a fine sense of humour, and was a splendid lecturer, enthusing her audience. By no means in old age, she passed away very suddenly ascending the stairs and was deeply mourned. Her several books brought her thoughts to everyone.

SIR FREDERICK STERN

Highdown

GORING-BY-SEA • SUSSEX

Worthing Borough Council

I MIGHT WELL QUOTE the old saying about an ill wind. It certainly was an ill wind that resulted in my catching scarlet fever in 1930 which caused me to spend my twenty-first birthday in a sanatorium. But this ill wind also led me to stay with a kind aunt at Littlehampton on the Sussex coast to recuperate. It was quite near to Arundel and its noble castle and Swanbourne Lake, and of course Highdown, the house of Major Stern (as he then was) and his already famous garden. With the cool effrontery of youth I cycled there with my aunt and rang the bell. Major Stern came to the door and, on my saying that I was from the Botanic Garden at Cambridge, he very kindly welcomed us and took us round his garden. It was a lovely morning in May and the garden was at its spring best with lilacs shedding their fragrance around, anemones, irises and a wealth of plants in flower, most but not all of which I knew. It was a wonderful experience and in subsequent visits through the next fifty years or more I was very grateful for his kindly friendship.

He was a man of great courage and determination and his garden in a chalkpit in the South Downs became a byword in horticultural circles as to what would thrive on chalk and what would not. For many years he was a member of Committee B at the Royal Horticultural Society and also a member of Council.

He captured many certificates for his plants, including several named after him, such as *Helleborus* x *sternii* and *Cotoneaster sternianus*.

In spite of having had no formal training in gardening, he became an expert at cultivating that difficult soil and many a lovely plant settled down and grew with a vigour that provided sheets of blossom. Some of his favourite plants were anemones, crocuses, irises, species and hybrids of *Eremurus*, peonies, daffodils, lilies and roses, with a great love also of shrubs of all kinds, and trees as well. His book, *A Chalk Garden* (1960) is an unrivalled textbook which is packed with pithy prose, enlarging succinctly on all aspects of his garden and plants. He also wrote definitive books on peonies and snowdrops.

A Chalk Garden contains a history of his experiments and takes us month by month through his amazing collection of plants. On reading it the novice will realize that there is no such thing as a 'dead month' in the year, but that all months are thoroughly enjoyable if one gardens intelligently. This he certainly did, having an able brain, an excellent memory, a great deal of 'drive' and a lovely sense of humour.

We came together particularly over roses, of which he grew a considerable selection. In the early days he used *Cupressus macrocarpa* as a windbreak, but they succumbed to a harsh winter and he busily started covering the shortened trunks with climbing, rambling and shrub roses. They were, many of them, struck from cuttings, because, although *Rosa canina*, the usual rootstock at the time, is a native of limy soils, it seemed to have an inability to serve as a stock on the chalk.

It was a plantsman's garden, on many different levels, with groups of beech and other trees breaking the views and providing some shelter from the souwesters.

Not only had he botanical leanings, but a scientific outlook as well; he loved raising plants from seeds, having many friends among gardeners in this country and around the world. Being manager of a large nursery at the time, I was also on the lookout for seeds of potential worth and spotted an entry for *Anemone pulsatilla* (now *Pulsatilla vulgaris*) 'Mrs Van der Elst' in Thompson and Morgan's seed catalogue soon after the Second World War. I had heard of this pink form but had never grown it. A packet of seeds produced a majority of pink forms of really good clear colouring. I took two or three to Fred Stern. He was surprised and delighted and I came away with young plants of *Paeonia emodi* and *P. veitchii*, which I still have.

He did not employ a large staff. One of his gardeners, Fisher by name, subsequently became Superintendent at Hampton Court and related to me how he had been suspended down the face of the chalk at the back of the pit in order to plant certain seedlings of shrubs and plants directly into the chalk face as an experiment. Some grew, others perished. Hoes were not used in the ornamental garden; weeds were controlled by hand with the result that interesting seedlings were preserved. One in particular has become famous, the rose 'Highdownensis', a seedling of *Rosa moyesii* with not only many flowers in bunches, but great drooping heads of large heps as well. I think the crowning glory was the sight of a flower of *Cypripedium calceolus* among the beech trees where the species had never been grown. I believe that they take about twelve years to flower from seed. Just think what would have happened if hoes had been used!

Fred Stern was a great lily grower and thanks to his industry and experiments we know something about which will tolerate the extreme chalky soil. *Lilium centifolium* was one of his triumphs. It grew six to seven feet and flowered regularly. From another source I secured two bulbs and they grew and flowered well for some six years but a frosty morning destroyed the young shoots when only about four inches high and I never saw them again. In his sun-trap garden they presented no difficulties.

Some years after the Hon. David Bowes-Lyon became President of the Royal Horticultural Society he was offered a knighthood, but it is said that he refused unless Fred could be offered one first. And so for his services to horticulture in so many ways he became Sir Frederick Stern, and well he deserved it.

On his death the garden was given to Worthing Borough Council with the desire that it should always be open free to visitors. His wife, Sybil, survived him by several years. I saw her at one of the RHS shows one day, and of course asked after the garden. She said, 'Quite colourful at the moment, but *they hoe.*'

LORD STRICKLAND

Sizergh Castle
KENDAL • CUMBRIA
National Trust

THE STRICKLAND FAMILY have lived at Sizergh for more than seven hundred years. Its garden owes much to Lord Strickland, who in 1926 built not only the terraces east of the house but also the rock garden which covers rather over half an acre on the north side. When I was advising on the garden half a century later only the back drive was used. Now the main drive takes you through the park past some very tall field maples.

In addition to the ancient tower, which dominates the whole area, there is a catchment area above the site, providing a seldom failing stream of water. It is used as a life giver to the rock garden and thence to a large pond and away into the countryside.

Lord Strickland employed the Ambleside firm of T.R. Hayes and Son to build the rock garden. I had long heard of this noted Lakeland firm; in fact the youngest member of the Hayes family had come to learn the craft of nurserywork for a year under me, shortly after the war. It therefore gave me much pleasure to find he remembered me many years afterwards.

There were few rock plants on the rock garden when I first visited; the area had proved too much and too involved for the one gardener, so we filled up many of the weedy areas with ground-covering plants. But it is not these that I want to write about, but the rich collection of dwarf conifers, many of which had made very large and good specimens, worth going a long way to see. Among them are immense specimens of piceas and abies; some are over eight feet across. And in the impressive area round the upper waterfall there is a very beautiful specimen of the Japanese pine, *Pinus parviflora*. There are many moisture-loving plants too: astilbes, calthas, primulas and *Darmera*. *Gentiana asclepiadea* seeds itself freely and has developed various blue and white forms. *G. acaulis* thrives under the castle wall.

I have not found out much about the last Lord Strickland, but he obviously had a great love for gardening and for plants in general, for he wisely left untouched a little knoll which is covered in native flowers through the early months of the year. Lent lilies (*Narcissus pseudonarcissus*) are followed by primroses, many wild orchids, dog daisies, campion and graceful grasses. Elsewhere there are sheets of pheasant's eye *Narcissus*.

There is also an eighteenth-century wall of stone faced with brick for the added warmth; it was originally a wall for trained fruit trees but is now given to a border of lovely shrubs and plants of world-wide origin. It runs along a terraced walk, ending in an arched niche and garden seat. After watching much beauty from flowers through the year, the tower in October caps it all for it goes out in a blaze of scarlet from *Ampelopsis*, so misleadingly called Boston ivy.

It is pleasant to add that two sisters, Alice and Kay Strickland, relatives of Lord Strickland, happened to join our madrigal group in Woking after the Second World War.

THOMAS UPCHER

Sheringham Park
NORFOLK
National Trust

FROM GREAT PROWESS in all kinds of sport and athletics, particularly cricket and running, my father turned to golf in his middle age. After sitting in an office all day throughout the year, no doubt he needed the freedom of the open air of golf courses to rejuvenate him at weekends and in the holidays. He continued playing golf until his eightieth year had passed. This may seem irrelevant to this book, but it meant he took his annual holiday in the first fortnight of September – usually good weather. As our home was in Cambridge we were within easy reach by rail of the Norfolk coast and so we stayed wherever there was a good golf course: Cromer, West Runton, Hunstanton and Sheringham! While he was golfing every day my mother, brother and I explored the district on foot. The fact that it was always September meant that we did not visit Sheringham Park for its rhododendrons; in fact, coming as we did from limy Cambridgeshire, they were not familiar plants to any of us.

Sheringham Park has a long history. It is within about a mile of the sea and thus can be affected by cold winds, but the park is well wooded and hilly and provided Humphry Repton with an ideal setting for the house which he and his son John Adey Repton built for the Upchers of the time. The new house was to be sheltered from the sea and hillocks were removed by hand implements, with carts and horses of course, from 1812 onwards, to provide pleasant views of the house from the approach drive. Horticulturally it was soon enriched by a planting of species and hardy hybrid rhododendrons in a nearby valley, a tradition that has continued. So there, within less than a mile of the sea, rhododendrons flourished and continued to get larger and more impressive.

Thomas Upcher inherited the property in 1954. He not only added greatly to the rhododendron collection, numbered in their hundreds and supplied by the Woking nurseries, but took shares in E.H. Wilson's expeditions to western China and the Himalaya and thus raised many species to add to the plantings. He also enriched the whole area with many trees and shrubs, including the handkerchief tree (*Davidia*), species of *Pieris, Styrax, Eucryphia, Halesia*, and many kinds of maple (*Acer*).

I had the happy experience of going through the collections with him and noted how the rhododendrons benefited from frequent sea mists. Scattered trees and shrubs among the hillocks were enough to protect them from sea winds and to promote vigorous growth. The soil was mainly sandy, having been deposited there in hundreds of feet of thickness by the receding glaciers after the Ice Age.

CHARLES PAGET WADE

Snowshill Manor
STOW-ON-THE-WOLD • GLOUCESTERSHIRE
National Trust

CHARLES PAGET WADE, an architect and artist as well as a gardener, took collecting bygones very much to heart. Snowshill Manor stands very high in the Cotswolds – 750 feet in fact – and its title confirms that snow lies long in the folds of the hills. Not deterred by its dereliction and the accumulated junk in what had perhaps been a garden at one time, he set about clearing the whole place and restoring the many buildings and walls. When this was done and he had had time to think about it all, he designed one of the most charming small gardens in the country, of not more than two acres. It is on many different levels, guarded by low walls into compartments, each different from the next, and lit by the sun – or shaded – with the tinkle of water ever present.

The walls give a feeling of stability to the house which stands on quite a steep slope. The Cotswold stone is of the deep yellowish tint which is met in various parts of the chain of hills. As a contrast Wade liked plants of a blue, mauve and purple colouring and these tints cropped up in what became known as 'Wade blue' (and very closely copied at nearby Hidcote) and was found wherever paint was used on doors, seats, tubs and other carpentry. On a small terrace above a covered sconce in a wall is a garden seat in Wade blue; above it on the wall is a Nychthemeron, which if activated by electricity would show the path of the sun through the zodiac as well as the time. This is just one of the many special features that Wade gave to his unique little property, so generously given to the National Trust in 1951.

THE WALPOLES

Mount Usher
CO. WICKLOW • EIRE
Privately owned

It was kind of Lady Moore of Glasnevin who sent me first to Mount Usher. I had a deeply enjoyed afternoon there with Mr E.H. Walpole. He was the son of the original owner of the delightsome property who had built the house beside the swiftly flowing river Vartry all from the proceeds of a famous linen store in Dublin. E.H. Walpole gave the whole property a great fillip by continuing to build footbridges across the river to make access to all parts of the garden easy. The climate is mild and damp, and a fresh, cool, moist air pervades the garden, making the growing of certain shrubs, trees and plants easy. And there is always the sound of water flowing over the weirs, fed by streams from the Wicklow Hills. I remember being quite struck with the great variety of trees, shrubs and plants on my first visit, but the most memorable plant of all was, to me, an immense specimen of *Pinus montezumae*, some fifty feet high and clothed to the ground with its great bunches of silky-looking needles about ten inches long. The whole tree shimmered in every breath of air.

Though most of the river was straight, there was a bend where a grouping of old Scots pines with ferns and phormiums and a sinuous path gave a lovely effect. But wherever you went or looked there was sure to be a specimen, or group, of something rare and beautiful.

The house was comparatively new, replacing the old mill house, and was tasteful and imposing among its many trees and shrubs. A special wall had been built with many large buttresses to try to capture every ray of sunshine for extra tender things. Although not a garden suited to roses, being too damp, one niche held a specimen of *Rosa* x *odorata* 'Pseudindica' or Fortune's Yellow. There were elsewhere sheets of *Gentiana verna*, far more luxuriant than on The Burren. There were hardy orchids in a great thick mass – I think *Dactylorhiza elata* 'Glasnevin' – and above us many species of *Eucalyptus* and conifers. One walk which acquired the name of the Rose Walk was given to a burst of hybrid azaleas followed by hydrangeas. Some other notable trees were *Populus wilsonii* with blue-green leaves, *Fagus engleriana*, *Abies koreana* with conspicuous blue cones, and *Abelia triflora*, about eighteen feet high. This is probably the tallest-growing abelia; many are small shrubs.

William Watson's famous nursery was at Killiney, near Dublin, and it was there that so many of the richly coloured brooms were raised, including the renowned 'Dorothy Walpole'. *Cytisus* x *dallimorei*, named after the foreman of the arboretum at Kew, was a cross between *C. multiflorus* and *C. scoparius* and practically all the brightly coloured brooms, 'Killiney this' and 'Killiney that', derive from this original cross.

I think we may say that Mount Usher owed much to the influence of William Robinson; there was scarcely a straight line anywhere and shrubs were placed informally. It was a most interesting garden, particularly when one was, as usual, escorted by E.H. Walpole. It is all well remembered in his two books entitled *Mount Usher*, where many of the trees, shrubs and plants are recorded. The garden was started by his forebear Edward in 1868 and the first of the two books carried the record on to 1928. The garden like all others suffered from neglect in the war, but E.H. infused it with new life and it was always in splendid condition when I visited – several times. For the second book E.H. asked me to contribute a chapter but I was too busy with the National Trust and had to refuse. Lanning Roper wrote it instead, following contributions by a string of Irish notabilities.

Unfortunately Robert Walpole, E.H.'s son, did not get enthused by the garden as a young man, so his father brought him over to England to see some famous gardens. I was delighted to hear they intended visiting me at Sunningdale Nursery and in my garden and we had what was to me a very happy day. But the times were not propitious for large gardens so Mount Usher was I believe made into a Trust and now has a tenant in the house. Robert came to live over here and we met on various occasions but, sadly, he died in 2001.

THE WARBURGS
Boidier
HEADLEY • EPSOM • SURREY
Privately owned

SIR OSCAR WARBURG brought up his family on the North Downs at a house called Boidier. Although not in the gardening profession, Oscar had strong horticultural leanings. He planted many conifers and other trees on his estate, but is chiefly remembered for his deep interest in the genus *Cistus*. Much of what we know of them today is founded on his investigations. He travelled to many islands and countries around the Mediterranean and introduced us to many forms and hybrids such as *Cistus x aguilarii* and a prostrate form of *C. salviifolius*. With him on his travels he took his eldest son, Edmund F. Warburg, who attended some of the botany lectures with me, and was a frequent visitor to the Cambridge Botanic Garden where I was working. He also became bitten with *Cistus*.

After I had transferred my attention to nursery work in Surrey, I got in touch and was delighted to receive an invitation to Boidier. It was not all conifers and cistuses! Edmund had a wide appreciation of plants, was a skilled botanist and became, with A.R. Clapham and T.G. Tutin, a joint author of *The Flora of the British Isles* in after years.

To my astonishment, in his special frames and beds were primulas of many kinds and alpine plants galore. But my memory specially lights on *Omphalogramma (Primula) vinciflora*, which must have benefited from the cool nights on the Downs. It was a plant I had read about but never seen; it is usually found in northern gardens. It was a thrilling sight to see it in flower. Edmund had, like his father, already visited many European countries and had a group of foot-high *Quercus coccifera* from seed collected on Mount Athos (shades of Dumas and *The Three Musketeers!*) in Greece. This I knew from a six-foot-high specimen at Cambridge and I had been confronted by a great specimen, about fifteen foot high, on William King's nursery near Camberley. (It was said that this was his 'test plant' to let him know whether a visitor was worth taking round.) Later I found a good young tree at Hidcote. It is more like a holly than an oak until you find an acorn. But it is a slow-growing rarity. There is an oak in the Botanic Garden at Cambridge which was never properly identified and labelled. Edmund set about it and it was eventually labelled *Quercus* 'Warburgii'. It is a noble tree, probably of hybrid origin, and has as its fellow another at Kew, though considerably smaller.

Edmund was a large man and became known by his family and friends as the Heffalump, shortened to Heff, from A.A. Milne's book. [The double snowdrop *Galanthus* 'Heffalump' is named after him.] But he left the Cambridge area and went to Oxford where in due course he became Professor of Botany, and married Primrose. They lived at Yarnell's Hill, overlooking the Dreaming Spires. Primrose was a keen gardener and knew Nancy Lindsay, from whom she acquired an enthusiasm for old French roses, and in later years I met her now and again at Mottisfont. They had an intriguing garden on a hilltop, sloping down and up, and grew a wide variety of plants, both being enthusiasts. Sadly, Edmund died at an early age; but Primrose lived until recently, deeply immersed in plants.

SIR CLOUGH WILLIAMS-ELLIS

Plas Brondanw
PORTH MADOG • GWYNEDD • NORTH WALES
Trustees of the Second Portmeirion Foundation

ONE OF THE TREATS of staying with A.T. Johnson and his wife, Nora, every other year was that they always found some special outing for me apart from the joys of their own garden. They took me to Portmeirion, near Penrhyndeudraeth, where there was a breathtaking group of Italianate buildings, simulating a village, disposed here and there down the steep cliffs to the sea. Some were tucked into the cliff, others had some level ground to stand on; all were just such as one might find on the shores of the Mediterranean. The group was really of small houses or apartments which could be hired for holidays. It was obviously a successful venture as more buildings had been put up when I returned a few years later, including the 'town hall' constructed like many another of old masonry. Sir Clough was always on the lookout for architectural pieces which he welded into picturesque realizations – including the masts and deck of a ship, apparently at anchor in the estuary. Many of the buildings had individual gardens, pools, terraces and so on, just as one might find in the Cotswolds or other hilly country.

Sir Clough was a gifted architect with a very fertile imagination. I did not have the good fortune to meet him, but after visiting Portmeirion several times while it was growing I

wrote to ask whether I might come and see his garden. I had a
most cordial letter in return, bidding me welcome when next in
Wales, but regretting he could not meet me there. His home
was inherited in a rather dilapidated state, having been built by
his forebears of four generations ago in a scenically wonderful
part of Wales. In creating a garden around it he took the fullest
advantage of the scenery. It included carefully selected views of
Snowdonia and a beautiful small peak, Cnicht. To accentuate
the natural scenery the planting was almost entirely done with
evergreens, often clipped into hedges and other shapes. The
solid granite house and local scenery did not need flowers but
some big clumps of hydrangeas and other solid things were
planted to compete with the stunning views. It gave me a whole
afternoon's pleasure.

ELLEN ANN WILLMOTT

Warley Place
GREAT WARLEY • ESSEX
Essex Wildlife Trust

I HAD BEEN FAMILIAR with the name of Willmott from early
days at Cambridge because it was to be found on so many
labels with her accession number. Miss Willmott was one of
the three people who dominated ornamental outdoor
gardening in the early part of the century. The others were of
course Gertrude Jekyll and William Robinson; only the last
named had any training in horticulture. I have written fully

about Ellen Willmott elsewhere (*A Garden of Roses*, 1987) but this book would not be complete without her. While it is true that she had wealthy parents who purchased Warley Place at Great Warley in Essex, the family moneys were little compared with the sum she inherited from her godmother – the Countess Tasker – at the age of thirty. In today's money that would amount to little short of five million pounds.

She was therefore able to indulge herself fully in her favourite pursuits of gardening and music. She was unusually talented, a singer and an instrumentalist and a lover of antique furniture and silver who spoke four languages. She was still singing in the Bach Choir just prior to her death in 1934 at the age of seventy-six. As if Warley Place was not enough for her, she purchased a house and garden at Menton and also at Ventimiglia, where she grew many exotics. She entertained royalty but her apparently bottomless pit of gold gave out and she died bankrupt. She could not stop spending.

Her love of beauty was extended particularly towards gardening but she also had a scientific turn of mind which tended to botany, though it did not diminish her devotion to her gardens. Late in her life she decided to rival the Empress Josephine (Napoleon's wife) in recording her collection of roses. She chose the renowned and gifted artist Alfred Parsons, who produced superlative paintings, particularly lifelike, but the colour printing and the binding of the two great volumes of *The Genus Rosa* were not good, and their appearance just before the Great War militated against sales. The unsold volumes were remaindered just before the Second World War and I purchased the set for £6 and thought myself very lucky.

To my regret I did not meet Miss Willmott nor did I see her garden until a few years ago. Russell Coates had business to do in the area and we went together. It was spring and we were greeted by millions of the genuine species of *Crocus vernus* in the surrounds of the garden, a fantastic sight, sheets and sheets of royal purple. The house had been pulled down. There were a few garden walls and many snowdrops and scillas, and signs of bluebells for later weeks. The great artificial valley of the rock garden, built of millstone grit by the famous firm of Backhouse of York, was intact but overgrown. There were a few common bamboos here and there and large mats of *Hedera colchica* and that was all apart from multitudes of sycamore seedlings.

Miss Willmott's sister Rose was also interested in gardening and married Robert J. Berkeley of Spetchley Park, Worcestershire. I did not meet her for she died early in life, but Robert and I had much in common and I stayed with him and his daughter once and saw the exquisite paintings by Parsons of the Warley garden which hang there. There is no doubt that Ellen's garden was very beautiful. The paintings are so 'alive' that it was almost like being there. It was tended by over a hundred gardeners, the bulk of whom were paid eighteen shillings a week; there was a large house staff as well.

Berkeley Castle, Avon, was Robert's also, with a very historic terraced garden. On one of the south-facing walls was the finest specimen I have ever seen of *Rosa* x *hardyi* (now *R* x *hulthemosa* x *hardyi*), no doubt a present from Warley. It was about five foot high and wide. I have never succeeded in growing it but it was well represented at Cambridge in the 1920s, along with *R. stellata*. It is bright yellow with red central zones. It was named after A.J. Hardy in 1836, who was keeper of the Luxembourg Gardens in Paris. It is good that his name is more readily remembered by the unsurpassed white damask rose, 'Madame Hardy' of 1832.

Ellen was a breeder of daffodils, just when the white varieties were coming to the fore, and also of tulips; in fact, until recently, the best pale yellow cottage tulip, 'Ellen Willmott', was grown regularly at Tintinhull, Somerset, and elsewhere. *Ceratostigma willmottianum* and *Rosa gymnocarpa* var. *willmottiae* testify to her prowess, as also do such plants as *Aethionema* 'Warley Rose' and 'Warley Ruber'. Every year she issued a seed list, containing as many as six hundred names of plants, which was sent out to botanic and other gardens.

She sat on several of the Royal Horticultural Society committees, had scientific and other volumes dedicated to her and kept up a voluminous correspondence in her own longhand with many famous botanists and gardeners of the day. Gertrude Jekyll, never given to irresponsible opinions, wrote that Ellen was 'the greatest of all living woman gardeners'. They were the only two women to be honoured with the RHS Victoria Medal of Honour when it was first awarded to commemorate the Queen's Diamond Jubilee.

CONCLUSION

No costly jewellery, no gift book, no picture serves so sweet as a living bush or herb to bring an absent friend to mind, and life without friends would be more desolate than a garden with neither flowers nor fruit.

Sir Herbert Maxwell, Bt., *Flowers, a Garden Notebook* (1923)

I HAVE COME TO AN END OF MY LIST but it has left a large number of gardens unrecorded. This is due partly to so many being the outcome of successive enthusiastic owners; they were not created and enjoyed in just the twentieth century which is what this book is about.

There is for instance the great subtropical garden on Tresco, in the Isles of Scilly. Its long period of development, still proceeding, prevents its inclusion in these pages. The Dorrien Smith family have been its designers and planters for several generations. My one and only visit was in August some years ago and I was entranced by all I saw, taken round by the then owner. The blue of African lilies was everywhere, including the seashore where they had spread by seed. The scarlet flowers of *Eucalyptus ficifolia* were a real eye-opener, and rows of Belladonna lilies were all about. I always wished to go again but the opportunity never occurred: there are so many great gardens in these islands.

Cornwall alone has a big gathering of gardens. Many are ancient – a product of the prosperous tin-mining age. I have only visited a few. One most splendid and richly planted is Trewithen at Grampound Road where G.H. Johnstone did so much planting of newly introduced rhododendrons, magnolias and innumerable other beautiful shrubs and trees. He gave us the fruits of his knowledge in a book on magnolias. His wife, Alison, planted what must have been the most far westerly rose garden; she has a subtly tinted, bell-shaped rhododendron named after her. I remember Mr Johnstone telling me of an extraordinary happening: he was having his breakfast one morning and looking out upon the close-mown lawn saw a cow vanish into thin air before his eyes. An underground passage, a long-forgotten relic of smuggling days, had given way, and lawn and cow had fallen out of sight!

Many great gardens in Cornwall have become neglected or have even practically disappeared. I have recalled one which has been faithfully restored – Heligan. But there were still wealthy owners who subscribed to the great expeditions to eastern Asia, and fortunately the climate of Cornwall and the west of Scotland and Ireland provided suitable conditions for so many of the plants introduced by the adventurous collectors of seed. And I believe that the raising of generations of seeds of these plants in this country has resulted in their adopting our country as a little bit of their motherland and getting used to our climate.

Something of the same sort happened in Ireland where the soft climate has suited the many shrubs and trees from the southern hemisphere, and especially Tasmania, whence Lord Talbot de Malahide, at Malahide Castle near Dublin, educated us so well in the native flora. And Sidney Maskell and his wife at Kilbogget, also near Dublin, created a very charming garden with a lawn sloping down from the house well planted around the perimeters with good trees and shrubs. The view from the little terrace (where one could walk on a silver carpet of *Raoulia*) towards the church tower and the distant Wicklow hills was delightful. The climate in the east of Ireland is very much drier than that of the south and west, which approximates closely to parts of Cornwall.

We pass Bodnant on the way to Scotland and I have given due space to Brodick and Logan. Next door to Logan is historic Lochinch which I always feel is the prime example of the use of rhododendrons in these islands. They are so well spaced. The historic garden with its wonderful specimens of *Embothrium* and *Cornus* and the ruined castle are a stunning sight. Penetrating the western highlands of Scotland, there is first renowned Crarae in Argyll, lavishly planted by Sir George Campbell. The gushing brook – even river – flows between rocks and pines, and a selection of notable specimen shrubs and trees makes this one of the most remarkable of Scottish gardens in the west. Gigha is farther on and like Inverewe depended for its inception on an early planting of shelter-belts. Here Sir James Horlick developed yet another garden in the Scottish scenic style. And so we go on to famous Inverewe with all its horticultural glories, to say nothing of the rainfall and the midges!

Two gardens on the east coast of Scotland deserve a mention. Unlike most big gardens, Pitmedden has a comparatively small house, certainly not one which would have had an army of servants and retainers to feed. As a consequence it seems that at least half of the garden area would have been devoted to a parterre, which was the way to display flowers in the late seventeenth century. Today it is like a superb picture in a delightful frame – the old walls, the corner pavilions with their graceful roofs and the intriguing central steps leading down from the upper slope. When the Scottish National Trust accepted the property the upper part was solid with trees and the lower portion – now the Great Garden – a market garden filled with plants and bushes.

The inspiration to develop a traditional parterre in this lower garden came from three old engravings of Holyrood House, Edinburgh, and the fourth admirably commemorates Sir Alexander Seton's coat of arms of about 1675. The whole conception has been so splendidly maintained with its annual bedding of thousands of dwarf colourful plants that I was not surprised one day to hear someone call it the Trust's flagship.

Surrounded by many castles and historic palaces, with the city of Perth as a centre and Bannockburn not far away, Falkland Palace has a long and involved history, being the place of rest and enjoyment for the royal families. It is set in lovely countryside, hilly and partly wooded, with the houses and cottages of the Royal Burgh nestling under it, right up to the walls on the entrance side. Its bulk and turrets dominate everything. It is now lived in by the Crichton-Stuart family, who have done so much to make it very pleasantly habitable with a lovely garden surrounding it on two sides, on various levels.

Being possibly somewhat daunted by the garden, which was at a low ebb at the end of the Second World War, they employed Percy Cane to make suggestions for its reinstatement and improvement. With so large a building dominating everything it had to be spacious and this was just what we had all come to expect from Cane. No spotty planting and petty effects from him, even if his predilection for flat-growing junipers did always creep in! The result is a garden of majesty, befitting the great building of warm-coloured sandstone.

I suppose it might be said that the superb natural scenery of the west of Scotland initially inspired people to go and settle there, but I have a feeling I should not want to make a garden where the scenery itself is so inspiring. Are not gardens a little *de trop*? Do not rocks and water, pines and birches provide enough beauty to satisfy us? One brilliant day a friend and I decided to climb to the top of the highest of the Sisters of Kintail. On reaching the crest we found that the skies had lifted and we could see the whole of the mountain tops stretching before us, from south to north, with only the Cairngorms still under cloud. Skye was also visible. Ascending a mountain is of course a very different matter from walking in a garden but there is much to be said for the former.

All the way we have travelled from the tip of Cornwall to Wester Ross the climate has been tempered by the North Atlantic Drift, hitherto called the Gulf Stream, and in fact it benefits our climate right round Scotland and as far south as the coast of Lincolnshire. The Gulf Stream branches off in mid-Atlantic and goes north to Iceland. Thus are the British Isles warmed and life made acceptable through the year, whereas other parts of the world at the same latitude – Poland, Hudson's Bay and the like – are frozen hard in winter. Much of this temperate climate has been responsible for our love of gardening.

REPRIEVE

A bell is ringing in my ears.
What does it mean?
Is it my passing bell
Ringing to tell
That I must leave a scene
I have loved long and well?

For it is winter now,
And I desire sweet spring –
And then the summer soon to be –
And then – Oh, let me see
One little autumn thing,
The red fruit on the spindle tree!

Sir William Beach Thomas
The Poems of a Countryman (1945)

Graham Stuart Thomas died on 17 April 2003

INDEX

Page numbers in italics refer to illustrations

Abbotswood, Stow-on-the-Wold, Gloucestershire 109–11
Aberconway, Lord (1913–2003) 60–2
Acland, Cuthbert Henry Dyke ('Cubby') 62–4, 167, 181
Allam, Jack 116, 118
Ampfield House, Romsey, Hampshire 123–5
Anglesey Abbey, Cambridgeshire 90–2
Anley, Gwendolyn (d. 1968) 65, 70–6, 84, 116
Ardsallagh, Tipperary, Eire 104–6
Armytage-Moore, Hugh (d. 1954) 74, 76–9
Astor, Lord ('Bill') 32
Astor, Waldorf 32

Ballard, Ernest 52
Batemans 46
Beech Park, Co. Dublin, Eire 217–19
Bean, W.J. 51
Benenden, Kent 127–9
Binny, Diany, 192, 193
Birch Farm Nursery 54, 56
Birr Castle, Co. Offaly, Eire 176
Blenheim Palace 47
Blickling Hall 20, 38, 46
Blythe, Tom 76, 77, 183
Bodnant, Colwyn Bay, North Wales 60–2
Boidier, Epsom, Surrey 241–2
Bolitho, Simon 36–7
Bolitho, Lt.-Col. Sir Edward Hoblyn Warren (1882–1969) 80–3
Bond, John 124, 216
Borlase, Peter 16, 36
Boscawen, Canon 81
Boscawen, Major J.P.T. 181
Bowes-Lyon, The Hon. David 214, 233
Bowles, Edward Augustus (1865–1954) 83–7, 117, 124, 207
Branklyn, Perth, Scotland 201–5
Brodrick Castle, Isle of Arran, Scotland 181–3
Broughton, Major Henry Rogers, 2nd Baron Fairhaven 88–9
Broughton, Huttleston, 1st Baron Fairhaven 88, 90–2
Brown, Rosemary 104, 197, 217
Buchanan-Hepburn, Agnes 171

Bulkeley Mill, Ty'n-y-Groes, North Wales 142–9
Bunyard, Edward A. 176–7
Burnett of Leys, Major-General Sir James Lauderdale Gilbert, 13th Baronet (1880–1953) 93–5
Burnett of Leys, Sibyl, Lady 46, 93–5, 189
Burrows, Geoff 39
Burrows, George Harry 39, 151
Bury, Lady Mairi 162
Buscot Park, Berkshire 198

Cambridge, University Botanic Garden 118–20
Campbell, Sir George 250
Cane, Percy 103, 251
Carwright-Hignett, Mrs. E. 197
Casson, Sir Hugh 115
Castle Howard, Yorkshire 77, 210–11
Chambers, Mr and Mrs J. 190
Chelsea Flower Show 51, 52, 54, 72, 107
Chertsey, Surrey 116–18
Chetwode Manor, Buckingham 112–14
Choate, Joseph 170–1
Claremont 28–9
Clarke, Sir Robert and Lady 135
Cliveden 17, 29, 31–3
Coates, Russell 245–6
Collins, Tim and Jennifer 114
Comber, James 176, 178
Cotehele 36
Cotton, Philip 14–15, 17, 31
Cox, E.H.M. 49, 107, 155
Crathes Castle, Kincardineshire, Scotland 46, 93–5, 196

Daisy Hill Nursery, Co. Down, Northern Ireland 183, 226
Dartington Hall, Totnes, Devon 102–4
Deeping, (George) Warwick (1877–1950) 96-8
Deeping, (Maude) Phyllis (d. 1971) 96-8
Dillon, Helen 104, 197, 219
Drury, Martin 28, 42
Dublin, National Botanic Gardens 184
Duchêne, Achille 47
Duncan, Geordie 202, 203, 204
Dutton, Ralph Stawell, 8
Baron Sherborne (1898–1985) 26, 99–101

East Riddlesden Hall 41
Eastlands, Weybridge, Surrey 96–8
Elizabeth, Queen Mother 57, 214
Elliott, Clarence 54, 107
Elmhirst, Leonard (1893–1974) 102–4
Elmhirst, Dorothy (1887–1968) 102–4
Elwes, H.J. 51
Essex Wildlife Trust: Warley Place 244–7

Fairhaven Woodland and Water Garden, South Walsham, Norfolk 88–9
Farquhar, Betty 104–6
Farrand, Beatrix 103
Farrer, Reginald (1880–1920) 49, 51, 106–8
Fedden, Robin 26
Fenwick, Mark (1860–1945) 109–11
Fforde, Lady Jean 183
Findlay, Thomas Hope 216
Fisher, Mark 206
Fleischmann, Ruby 111, 112–14, 189
Forestry Commission: Gravetye Manor 205–9; Westonbirt Arboretum 178–80
Forrest, George 49, 51
Fox, Dr Wilfred Stephen (1875–1962) 114–15

Galsworthy, Frank (b. 1863) 116–18
Garden History Society 25, 26
Gearing, Arthur 128
Getty, J. Paul 139
Gilbert-Carter, Humphrey 118, 119
Gilmour, John Scott Lennox (1906–86) 118–20
Gilpin, William Sawrey 126
Glyndebourne Festival Opera 65, 75
Gould, Norman H. 84, 124
Gravetye Manor, East Grinstead, Sussex 205–9
Guincho, Co. Down, Northern Ireland 163–4
Guthrie, L. Rome 47

Haddington, Earl of (1894–1986) 121–2
Haddington, Countess of 121–2
Hadfield, Miles 26, 26–7

Hancock, Jimmy 35
Hardy, A.J. 246
Hascombe Court, Godalming,
Surrey 134–5
Hay, Thomas 51, 124
Hayes, R.T. & Son 234
Headfort, Marquess of 49, 50
Heale House, Wiltshire 198
Heathcoat-Amory, Sir John
(1894–1922) 65–9
Heathcoat-Amory, Joyce, Lady
(1907–97) 65–9
Heligan Gardens, St Austell,
Cornwall 220–2, 249
Herbert, Peter 206, 207
Hestercombe 46
Hidcote Manor, Chipping Camden,
Gloucestershire 39–40, 46,
150–4, 196, 238, 242
Highdown, Goring-by-Sea, Sussex
230–3
Hillier & Son 52, 54, 123
Hillier, Sir Harold 123–5
Hilling, T. & Co. 11, 12, 210
Hinton Ampner, Alresford,
Hampshire 99–101
Howard, George 211
Hume, Rosemary 229
Humphris, John 141
Hussey, Christopher Edward Clive
(1899–1970) 125-7
Hussey, Betty 125-7

Ilford Manor, Wiltshire 197–8
Illustrations: *Anemone* x *hybrida*
'Honorine Jobert', *A.* x *h.*
'Prinz Heinrich' *3*; *Erythronium dens-canis*,
E. 'Pagoda' *204*; *Eucryphia* x
nymansensis 'Nymansay' *177*;
Galanthus caucasicus, *G.* 'Magnet',
G. nivalis 'Plenus', *G.n.* 'Scharlokii',
G.n. 'Straffan' *73*; *Gentiana
asclepiadea* 'Knightshayes' *66*;
Gentiana farreri *108*, *108*;
Helleborus Bowles's Yellow' *85*;
I. missouriensis *59*; *Iris unguicularis*,
I. u. 'Mary Barnard' *3*; *Magnolia* x
thompsoniana *81*; *Meconopsis* x
sheldonii 'Slieve Donard' *218*;
Prunus mome 'Omoi-no-mama' *3*;
Rhododendron 'Cilpinense', *Rh.*
'Praecox', *Rh.* 'Ptarmigan' *208*;
Rh. moupinense *215*; *Rosa* 'Bobbie
James' *133*; *R. filipes* 'Kiftsgate'
193; *R.* 'Lawrence Johnston' *153*;
R. 'Sissinghurst Castle' *195*;
R. stellata var. *mirifica* *186*; *R.* 'Bleu
Magenta', *R.* 'Goldfinch',
R. 'Rose-Marie-Viaud', *R.*
'Veilchenblau', *R.* 'Violette', *227*

Ingleborough, Yorkshire 106–8
Ingram, Collingwood ('Cherry')
127–9
Ingwersen, W.E.Th. 54, 56, 145
Ishlan, Co. Antrim, Northern
Ireland 212–13
Iveagh, Earl of (1874–1967)
129–30
Iveagh, Countess of (1881–1966)

James, Lady Serena 134
James, The Hon. Robert
(1873–1960) 131–4
Jarvis, Sir (Joseph) John 134–5
Jekyll, Gertrude (1843–1932) 46,
94, 130, 135–8, 139, 140, 141,
146, 207, 244, 246;
GT designs in style of 34, 35, 37,
42
Jellicoe, Sir Geoffrey Alan (b. 1900)
and Susan 139–41
Jenkinson, R.C.H. (Bobby) 112,
155, 156
John Innes Institute 48
Johnson, Arthur Tysilio
(1873–1956) 60, 142–9, 202,
243
Johnson, Nora 142–9
Johnston, Lawrence (d. 1957) 46,
150–4, 190
Jones, Colin 27, 151
Jones, Gavin 56, 107

Keillour Castle, Perthshire, Scotland
158–9
Kiftsgate Court, Chipping Camden,
Gloucestershire 190–3
Killerton, Devon 30, 37, 62, 63, 68
Kipling, Sir Rudyard 46
Knap Hill Nursery, Surrey 52,
154–7
Knight, Frank P. 11, 124, 154–7
Knightshayes Court, Tiverton, Devon
65–9
Knox Finlay, Major and Mrs 158–9
Kreutzberger, Sibylle 40, 194

Lee Valley Regional Park Authority:
Myddelton House, Enfield,
Middlesex 83–7
Lilley, Jack 36
Lindsay, Nancy 39, 242
Lindsay, Norah 47
Little Moreton Hall 26
Lloyd, Christopher 42
Logan, Wigtownshire, Scotland
171–3
Londonderry, Marchioness of 46,
160–3
Long Ashton 48

Lutyens, Sir Edwin 46, 110, 134
Lyme Park 38–9

Mackie, Vera 163–4
Malahide, Lord Talbot de 249
Mansfield, Peter 28, 29, 37
Marchant, W.J. 145
Marshall, Nigel 15, 31, 162
Mary, Queen 214
Maskell, Sidney 249–50
Mason, L. Maurice and Margaret
165–7
Mawson, T.H. 46
Maxwell, Bernard 167–9
Maxwell, Sir Herbert Eustace
169–71, 248
McDouall, Kenneth and Douglas
171–3
Messel, Anne 176
Messel, Leonard 174
Messel, Maud 112, 174
Mitchell, Anthony 18, 27
Mitchell, W.J. 178–80
Moerheim Nursery 148
Monreith, Wigtownshire, Scotland
169–71
Montacute House 11, 201
Montrose, Mary Louise, Sixth
Duchess of 181–3
Moon, Geoffrey 14, 33–4
Moore, Phyllis, Lady (d. 1974)
183–9, 238
Moore, Sir Frederick 183–4
Morris, Sir Cedric 74
Moseley Old Hall 25–6
Mottisfont 41–2
Mount Stewart, Co.Down, Northern
Ireland 31, 46, 160–3
Mount Usher, Co.Wicklow, Eire
238–40
Muir, Heather Agnes 46, 190–3
Munstead Wood, Godalming, Surrey
135–8
Myddelton House, Enfield,
Middlesex 83–7

National Trust 10–13, 22ff., 101;
gardens: Anglesey Abbey,
Cambridgeshire 90–2; Bodnant,
Colwyn Bay, North Wales 60–2;
Eastlands, Weybridge, Surrey 96-
8; Hidcote Manor, Chipping
Camden, Gloucestershire 39–40,
46, 150–4; Hinton Ampner,
Alresford, Hampshire 99–101;
Knightshayes Court, Tiverton,
Devon 65–9; Mount Stewart,
Co. Down, Northern Ireland 31,
46, 160–3; Nymans, Handcross,
Sussex 174–8; Rowallane, Co.

Down, Northern Ireland 76–9;
Scotney Castle, Lamberhurst,
Kent 125–7; Sheringham Park,
Norfolk 235–7; Sissinghurst
Castle, Cranbrook, Kent 194–6;
Sizergh Castle, Kendal, Cumbria
233–5; Snowshill Manor, Stow-
on-the-Wold, Gloucestershire
237–8; 150–1; Stagshaw,
Ambleside, Cumberland 62–4;
Tintinhull, Yeovil, Somerset
199–201; Trengwainton,
Penzance, Cornwall 80–3;
Winkworth Arboretum,
Godalming, Surrey 114–15
National Trust for Scotland
Branklyn, Perth 201–5; Brodrick
Castle, Isle of Arran 181–3;
Crathes Castle, Kincardineshire
93–5; Pitmedden, Grampian
250–1
Nelson, Charles 176, 197, 212
Nicoll, John 172
Nicolson, Sir Harold (1886–1968)
194–6
Notcutts 52, 157
Nymans, Handcross, Sussex 174–8,
198

Peto, Harold Ainsworth
(1854–1933) 197–8
Pitmedden, Grampian, Scotland
250–1
Plas Brondanw, Gwynnedd, North
Wales 243–4
Polesden Lacey, Surrey 62
Powis, Powys, Wales 35
Pyrford Court, Woking, Surrey
129–30

Quest-Ritson, Charles 42

Reiss, Phyllis (d. 1961) 46,
199–201
Renton, John and Dorothy 201–5
Repton, Humphry 236
Robinson, William (1838-1935)
46, 138, 146, 205–9, 240, 244
Rogers, Michael 32
Roper, Lanning 24, 29, 240
Rosse, Earl of 27–8, 174, 176
Rothamsted 48
Rothschild, Lionel de 54, 155
Rowallane, Co. Down, Northern
Ireland 76–9
Rowley, Sir Joshua 65, 68
Royal Horticultural Society 48, 51,
60, 61, 83–4, 124, 131, 157,
158–9, 165, 192, 231, 247
Russell, George 52

Russell, James Philip Cumming
(1920–1996) 41, 42, 77, 111,
209–12
Ruys, B. 148

Sackville-West, Vita (1892–1962)
194–6, 201
St George's, Woking, Surrey 70–6
St Nicholas, Richmond, Yorkshire
131–4
Saltram 37–8
Sanderson, Molly and Noel 212–13
Savill Garden, Windsor Great Park,
Berkshire 214–17
Savill, Sir Eric Humphrey
(1895–1980) 214–16
Schwerdt, Pamela 40, 194
Scotney Castle, Lamberhurst, Kent
125–7
Scott, John 200
Shackleton, David (1924–1988)
104, 217–19
Sherborne, Lord (Ralph Dutton)
26, 99–101
Sheringham Park, Norfolk 235–7
Sidney Sussex College, Cambridge
222–5
Sissinghurst Castle, Cranbrook, Kent
40–1, 194–6
Sizergh Castle, Kendal, Cumbria
233–5
Skinner, Archie 17, 33
Smit, Tim 220–2
Smith, B.T.D. 222–5
Snowshill Manor, Stow-on-the-
Wold, Gloucestershire 237–8
Spry, Constance (1886–1960)
225–9
Stagshaw, Ambleside, Cumberland
62–4
Steadstone, Kirkcudbrightshire,
Scotland 167–9
Stern, Sir Frederick Claude
(1884–1967) 50, 124, 230–3
Strickland, Lord (d. 1940) 233–5
Sunningdale Nursery, Windlesham,
Surrey 209–12, 215
Sutton Place, Guildford, Surrey
139–41
Sutton Place Foundation 139, 140,
141
Symons-Jeune, B.H.B. 55, 107

Talbot Manor, King's Lynn, Norfolk
165–7
Thomas, Sir William Beach, *The
Poems of a Countryman* 58, 253
Tintinhull, Yeovil, Somerset
199–201
Tipping, H. Avray 46, 103

Trengwainton, Penzance, Cornwall
36–7, 80–3
Tresco, Isles of Scilly 248
Tustin, Fred 109–11
Tyninghame, East Lothian,
Scotland 121–2

Ulster Gardens Scheme 163
University Botanic Garden,
Cambridge 118–20
Upcher, Thomas 235–7

Wade, Charles Paget (1883–1956)
237–8
Wall, Christopher 18, 25,31, 38
Wall, John 71, 201
Wallington 33–4
Walpole, Edward Horace
(1880–1964) 184, 223,
238–40
Waltham, T. Ernest 86, 106
Warburg, Edmund Frederic
(1908–66) 241–2
Warburg, (Phyllis) Primrose (d.
1996) 242
Warburg, Sir Oscar 241
Warley Place, Great Warley, Essex
244–7
Waterer, Anthony 54
Waterer, Donald 156, 157
Waterer, F. Gomer 155, 156, 157
Waterer's 52, 127, 128, 155
Waterfield, Aubrey 193
Waterperry 48
Wayford Manor, Somerset 198
West Dean Park, Sussex 198
Westbury Court 26–7
Weston, Sir Richard 139
Westonbirt Arboretum, Tetbury,
Gloucestershire 178–80
Wilbrook House, Dublin 183–9
Williams, J.C. 51, 81
Williams, P.D. 81
Williams-Ellis, Sir Bertram Clough
(1883–1978) 243–4
Wilmott, Ellen Ann (1858–1934)
55, 132, 244–7
Wilson, E.H. 236
Winkfield House, Windsor,
Berkshire 225–9
Winkworth Arboretum,
Godalming, Surrey 114–15
Woodall, Edward 185
Workman, John 11
Worthing Borough Council,
Highdown, Goring-by-Sea,
Sussex 230, 233
Wye College 48

Younger, Robert W. 120